Bureau of Prisons

Alcatraz
MOST WANTED

Profiles of the Most Famous Prisoners on the Rock

Cory Kincade

Ariel Vamp Press
Berkeley, California

A Most Happy Fella

Al Capone 1899 – 1947

During the peak of his life in the late 1920s, Al Capone could be seen climbing out of an armor-plated Cadillac with as many as 18 bodyguards piling out of nearby sedans.

He wore a cream-colored Borsalino hat, a full-length raccoon coat and highly polished shoes, a custom-made suit, monogrammed shirt and silk tie, and under everything—he bragged—Italian silk underwear. Of course his 11.5 caret diamond ring flashed as big as his smile.

He was a "walking tourist attraction," according to one of his biographers, Robert J. Schoenberg. He owned brothels, saloons, gambling houses, as many as eight full-scale breweries and he delivered the liquor using his own trucks. He could walk into a club that either he or a friend owned with an entourage of people, close the doors and announce that all drinks were on him. When the stock market crashed in 1929, ushering in the Great Depression, Capone opened a free soup kitchen.

He owned Chicago—the politicians, the cops, the witnesses, and the people who wanted to party—nobody could touch him. And he was only 30 years old.

Until then his life had unfolded like a perfect poker hand; every card lent power to the next. He was bright, organized, ruthless, glamorous, and Prohibition was his wild card.

Born in 1899 to Italian immigrants, Capone grew up in Brooklyn, New York, the fourth of eight children. In prison documents later, he drew a more sympathetic picture of his family than did his biographers. His eldest brother, the first born, left the family to go out west about 1914, became a sheriff and wasn't heard from for the next 20 years. Francis, the third born son, was killed in a never explained gun battle with police detectives. Capone claimed he was a newspaper delivery man shot by unknown persons. He also claimed that his father died when he was 14, forcing him to quit school to help support the family. But other sources say he quit school after a fight with his teacher and his father died when he was 20.

Whatever the truth, Capone's father—a first generation immigrant—may have been too busy feeding his family of 10 to notice his kids' shenanigans. Or, more likely given Capone's later ease with killing his rivals, and the troubled brothers, he may have been a demanding and cruel man.

As a teenager, Capone was a member of a neighborhood street gang, a rowdy group of boys whose deeds were more pranks than crimes. Local politicians took notice, however, because the kids could leaflet the neighborhood and get out the vote. Thus, the politicians overlooked some of the deeds of their young constituents. Capone grew up to be a ruthless man who craved attention and loved to please. His early lessons with these politicians became a lifelong model.

As he moved up from street thug to criminal, Capone joined the "Forty Thieves Juniors," a branch of an adult gang, the "Five Points," named after the notorious New York neighborhood. Two Five Points men, a kid named Frankie Yale, and the neighborhood idol, John Torrio, would shape his life.

Yale hired Capone as a bartender and bouncer in his establishment. Yale was a smooth, cruel man who dispensed

GGNRA/PARC GOGA-35178

GNRA/PARC GOGA-35173

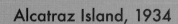

Alcatraz Island, 1934

Seen from Coit Tower (1), Alcatraz was an Army Disciplinary Barracks until 1933. The rock island was carved and paved over by Army prisoners (2). The cell house, at the top of the island, and the family housing along the parade ground, on the right, were also mostly built by military prisoners. Lieutenant Isaac Faulk, with his family (3), was one of the first federal employees to move onto the island in 1934. Alcatraz had its own post office to privately handle mail to and from prisoners.

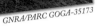

Courtesy of Ed Faulk

favors and money, but could beat his own brother badly enough to put him in a hospital, and as Capone would discover, betray his best friends. Capone would one day have him killed. "Terrible John" Torrio, a tiny, mousy man who looked more like an eccentric math professor than a gangster, was also brutal enough to extract fees from local pimps and gamblers, force shopkeepers to pay "protection" fees, collect dues for fixing prices and lend money to workmen at exorbitant interest rates. Initially, Capone could only admire him from a distance but that would change.

Capone had his share of trouble as a teenager. After he insulted a young woman, her brother, a local hood, pulled out a knife and sliced his left cheek. Local powers decreed that Capone was at fault and he never took revenge. That's what earned him the name "Scarface," although no one dared call him that to his face. That same year, 1918, he beat a man nearly to death. It was this attack and outside forces that would change his life.

A cousin of Torrio's was married to "Big Jim" Colosimo, a Chicago brothel owner who was having problems with rival gangs. He invited Torrio from New York to help eliminate his problems, and Torrio and two friends took care of it. The murders were never solved. Impressed, Colosimo offered Torrio a job managing part of his lucrative Chicago business and Torrio moved to Chicago.

Yale needed to get Capone out of town and away from the New York cops, so he asked Torrio if he could find a job for Capone. Torrio agreed and in 1919 Capone became "Terrible John's" protégé.

Capone was a hulking presence even then, 5'10", approaching 200 pounds, a young man with such enormous energy that Albert Best, who served on Alcatraz with him, later described him as putting "the *go* in ego." Under Torrio, Capone refined his intimidation tactics to include what cons called "the thousand-yard stare"—which combined with his willingness to kill—could leave anyone shaken.

By then, Capone had married his childhood sweetheart, Mae Coughlin, and had a son. He moved the family to Chicago, and within a few years his mother and younger siblings also moved in with him.

All was not well in the Capone household however. In 1919, while in the men's room one day, he noticed a lesion on his genitals, which must have left him shaken. It was the first sign of syphilis.

Although the lesion disappeared in a few days, within two months he probably developed a rash with clusters of red spots all over his body, including his hands and feet. This was frightening enough, but the long-term prognosis was even worse.

For 300 years syphilis had been one of the most dreaded diseases known to man, feared as much as AIDs is feared today. Often called the pox because of epidemics that swept through Europe as early as the 15th century, its spirochetes burrowed into various parts of the body, wreaking long-term havoc on the aorta, the brain, the eyes, the joints or the bones—often leading to misdiagnosis. In late stages of neurosyphilis, for example, the patient goes through euphoric and depressed cycles, leading to the misdiagnosis of manic-depression. Patients in secondary syphilis often lived for many years with debilitating headaches, agonizing body aches, or gastrointestinal cramps so severe they could leave a man crawling, weeping. Even worse, some people experienced *tabes dorsalis*, in which degenerating nerve endings led to severe pain and paralysis.

It was incurable in those pre-penicillin times. And although most wealthy Italians had large families in those days, Capone only had one child, a son born in 1918, a year before his diagnosis. Congenital syphilis was a real fear; a child born with it had minimal chance of a long life. Clearly, Capone and his wife decided against inflicting the disease onto the next generation. In fact, for the next two years, and for possibly many years after that, Capone could still be contagious. And although he would remain asymptomatic for the next decade or so, his disease was a death sentence.

The timing of his move to Chicago, however, couldn't have been better. By January 1920, the 18th Amendment had become law, forbidding the production, sale or transport of alcoholic beverages. For established criminals, it was like winning the lottery. But Colosimo feared bootlegging would lead to more killings and he wouldn't back Torrio's ambitious plan to purchase other breweries. Torrio was not going to let Colosimo stand in his way. He hired Capone who in turn hired Frankie Yale and before long Colosimo was dead. The murder was never solved.

That's how Capone got shares of the brothel, gambling, extortion and bootlegging business. As they purchased

> Alcatraz would be the most famous prison in America— Al Capone its most famous prisoner.

America's most famous

gangster. By March 1929 when this photograph was taken as he sat with attorney William F. Waugh, Capone was at the peak of his career and only 30 years old. Nearly ten years of Prohibition had made the Chicago mobster a rich man supplying liquor to a willing public. The Great Depression would begin in a few months, eventually throwing nearly a quarter of the population out of work. Capone opened free soup kitchens, his trucks delivered milk to school children, promoting his reputation as a "Robin Hood" kind of gangster. This was good publicity, of course, making Capone feel virtuous and keeping others indebted to him.

Chicago History Museum

more saloons, which required more liquor, he and Torrio grew fabulously wealthy. It was the Roaring Twenties, a large, young generation wanted to drink and party, and the highflying gangsters had the wind at their backs. They hired cops who could make more money in one night guarding a shipment than they made in a month on the force. Gangsters like Torrio and Capone spent nearly a million dollars a month for political and police protection. And those favors were returned.

But people get greedy when a lot of money is involved. By 1924, rival gangs increasingly were hijacking each other's shipments. And when the Thompson submachine gun appeared on the streets, Chicago began averaging one murder a day. Wags dubbed the new gun the "Chicago typewriter" not only because of the sound it made, but because of the ink it generated. Torrio could not keep the peace and after he was gunned down in 1925, he retired to Italy with grievous injuries. That left Capone, at age 26, as one of the most powerful men in Chicago in charge of much of the city's bootlegging operations. In a world where everyone who drank was an "outlaw," Capone became more glamorous than a movie star.

But the beginning of the end was at hand. George "Bugs" Moran, a Capone rival, was told that a big liquor shipment would arrive at his warehouse on February 14,

Capone was an icon in the 1920s and a model for gangsters in films and reality.

1929—St. Valentine's Day. That morning witnesses saw a police investigator's car pull up and five men—two in police uniforms—climb out of it. Later, people speculated that Moran's gang thought that this was a simple police shakedown and conveniently let the cops in. Within minutes, six of Moran's gang (and one unlucky visitor) were executed against a brick wall. But Moran was not among them; he showed up late for work that day. The two uniformed men then ushered the other three gang members out the door—hands held high as if under arrest—and the ruse was complete.

Real cops were livid. They rounded up the usual suspects, held inquests and even found the sedan, partially dismantled and burning. But they never solved the murders. Capone, the biggest beneficiary, was conveniently vacationing in Florida. Nonetheless, the massacre made him a nationally known figure. At the same time it turned the tide of public opinion against the gangsters, confirming that Prohibition created more crime than it solved.

The turn in American public opinion wasn't Capone's only problem, however. Filing yearly income tax reports had become law in 1927. Capone never filed, on the supposition that illegal earnings could not be taxed. But a 1927 Supreme Court ruling that illegal

1929 **FEBRUARY** 1929

(Check Spaces on "Important" Dates. Keep Record of "Important" Items on Record Pages.)

Sun

Chicago History Museum

The St. Valentine's Day Massacre

On February 14, 1929 six men lie dead and another died later after being executed by rivals masquerading as police officers (1). Capone was questioned by Chicago police (2) but he could prove he was in Miami at the time. His lieutenant, "Machine Gun" Jack McGurn, who is often credited with organizing the hit, had an alibi whom he later married; the media dubbed her the "blonde alibi." The murders were never solved. But Capone's troubles were only beginning; less than three years later he was going down for income tax evasion (3).

AP/Wide World Photos

AP/Wide World Photos

money was taxable provided a new tool with which to go after big time gangsters. (These were the years before the Omnibus Crime Act, or the Racketeering-Influenced and Corrupt Organizations Act, RICO, which netted many Mafia crime bosses in the 1980s and later. In the 1920s, income tax laws were the only way for federal agents to investigate gangsters and, more importantly, to testify against them.)

It took several years but the government was finally able to document that he had earned more than $1 million from 1924 to 1929—a ludicrously small estimate—and owed the U.S. government almost a quarter of a million dollars. Capone told everyone who would listen that he had been double-crossed; he had gone to investigators and offered to pay up and he had gotten the impression that that would take care of it. Instead, he was indicted. Then he claimed he had a deal with government attorneys to plead guilty in exchange for a light sentence. When the judge said there would be no deal, Capone pled not guilty. But he understood that his original plea weakened his case. He was tried, found guilty and on October 24, 1931, he was given a sentence of ten years in federal prison and one year in county jail. In the end, it was accountants who nailed Capone, not armed agents.

He was 33 when he arrived at the U.S. penitentiary in Atlanta and still acting like he was at the top of his game. As one warden later put it, he was by turns suave and aggressive. He worked in the shoe shop, which he found tedious. He also grumbled about the yard time, which was limited to 35 minutes twice a week. He thought he could sponsor professional fights among the inmates. Eventually he was able to compromise some officers through bribes or intimidation. He was suspected of getting mail and money into the prison, and it was generally thought he was still running his business through his lawyers.

At his intake evaluation his syphilis was thoroughly documented. "The right pupil is larger than the left," the report stated, "and does not react to light." He was also given the diagnosis as a psychopath without psychosis.

In 1934, the U.S. government opened Alcatraz as the most maximum security prison in the country. It was designed for troublemakers and big shots like Capone. That August, Capone and about 50 others from the Atlanta prison traveled by rail across the United States to Alcatraz. The train was dubbed the "Al Capone Special" and during the hot summer of 1934, with masses of

While Capone was housed in the U.S. penitentiary in Atlanta, Alcatraz Warden James A. Johnston (right) shows U.S. Attorney General Homer Cummings the newly selected officers. The federal prison on Alcatraz opened in August 1934 and Capone arrived the same month.

Welcome to "the Rock"

Americans were looking for a diversion in August 1934. The drought in the Midwest made it an unusually hot summer and the Great Depression was into its fifth year. Here ordinary citizens watch a passenger train enroute from Atlanta, Georgia to Alcatraz, California, dubbed the "Al Capone Special."

San Francisco Public Library

people out of work from the Great Depression, it seemed to symbolize the end of the Roaring Twenties and the crime-ridden Dirty Thirties.

Capone shuffled onto the dock as AZ #85. He was the most famous man to ever set foot on the most famous prison. But when photographed on August 22, 1934, he had a goofy grin on his round face, instead of his million dollar smile. At 5'10" and 255 pounds he looked more like comedian Fatty Arbuckle than a feared Chicago mobster.

"I didn't have any trouble picking him out when he was lined up for identification his first day," said James A. Johnston in his book, *Alcatraz Island Prison.* Johnston, who had been a reform-minded warden at California state prisons in his earlier years, did an about-face when hired as warden of Alcatraz. He wouldn't allow prisoners to talk in their cells, in the dining hall or while marching to and from work. Johnston's rule of silence would be controversial and would fall by 1938 after a series of strikes followed the death of a prisoner. "Before I called him to

the desk for instructions, I could see him nudging the prisoners and slipping them some corner-of-the-mouth comment. I signaled to him when it was his turn. As he walked toward me he flashed a big, wide smile."

Capone was prepared to wrap the warden around his finger as he had in Atlanta. And prison authorities were quite aware of his special status. He got telegrams from his family every time there was an incident on Alcatraz, requests from around the country for interviews (denied),

Alcatraz Alumni Association

NARA

Capone's mug shot the day he arrived on Alcatraz.

Warden James A. Johnston seemed to embody the government's get-tough policy on crime as he converted the military prison into a federal prison. Although previously a reform-minded administrator, his tenure on Alcatraz (1934-1948) was marked by the "silent system" for the first four years. Silence was difficult to enforce and finally abandoned in 1938. Ten (of fourteen) escape attempts occurred during his years, in which seven prisoners were fatally shot and three guards died—one officer by friendly fire.

UNITED STATES DEPARTMENT OF JUSTICE
FEDERAL BUREAU OF INVESTIGATION

TRANSFERRED TO FEDERAL CORRECTIONAL INSTITUTION, Terminal Island, JANUARY 6, 1939, Date of Birth 1/17/99

Name Alphonse Capone   No. 85   Color White Rec'd Aug.22,1934   From Atlanta   Age 35

Offense Violating Income Tax Laws.
Date of Sentence   Oct. 24, 1931
Sentence 10 years & $37,617.51 F.& G.
Sentence began   May 4, 1932
Minimum exp. date   Jan.19,1939
Maximum exp. date   May 3, 1942
Parole date (Denied) Sept. 3,1935

Good conduct credits   1200 days
Credits forfeited
Credits restored

District sentenced N/Ill. Chicago

Reason For Transfer
Subject is now serving sentence of 10 years for Violation of Income Tax Law. He is a notorious criminal, being a gang leader and racketeer. He has been suspected of clandestine correspondence, while confined at USP Atlanta, and of trying to have money transferred into the institution clandestinely. Transfer is recommended with Close Supervision.

DETAINERS Commitment reads that we are to safely deliver subject to the Cook Co. Jail, with a copy of writ, where he will serve sentence with reference to misdemeanors etc; Warrant filed Sept. 23, 1938, by Sheriff's office of Cook County, Ill., (Conspiracy)

Partners or co-defendants   x

Escape record or attempt to escape

Former Institutional Rule Violations
10-31-33---ISOLENCE:The above named prisoner was told by me to wash the window. I assigned one window to each member of the detail; every one including subject washed their window. After they had completed their work this prisoner became very insolent and wanted a pass to the Deputy Warden saying that he did not wash windows for anyone. This man created a lot of confusion amongst the detail when he started yelling out "did you see me wash that window". This is the second time he has become insolent to me in front of the rest of the detail. Action: Reprimanded and Warned

CRIMINAL HISTORY CONTINUED FROM BELOW:
5-8-30----Arrested in Miami,Fla;Suspicion; Released
2-27-31----Sentenced at Chicago,Ill; 6 months for contempt appealed the case;conviction affirmed (Part of this sentence)

Criminal History
1919---Arrested at New York City; Disorderly conduct. (Fighting) Discharged.
1923---Arrested in Chicago,Ill., Traffic Violation; (Collision) Dismissed.
1923--(Denies) Fined $150;Operating disorderly house; Gambling at Chicago.Ill.
9-5-23----Arrested with pistol in car;Discharged.
3-5-24----Arrested in Chicago,Ill;witness of murder;Released
1925----Arrested in Olean,N.Y.,Disorderly;Released(Denied)
6-7-26----Indicted in Chicago;Vio.N.F.A. Dismissed.
7-15-26---Indicted in Stickney,Ill.,Vote fraud;Dismissed
7-28-26---Arrested in Chicago; Murder; Charge withdrawn
10-1-26---Indicted in Chicago;V.N.P.A.(26 others)dismissed
11-18-27--Arrested in Chicago;Refusal to testify;Dismissed
12-22-27--Fined $2600,Joliet,Ill;(5 other henchmen)Con.Weap
5-17-29---Received at Eastern State Penitentiary,Phila,Pa. Chg:concealed weapon;Discharged by exp. 3-17-30
1928------Arrested in Miami,Fla; Suspicion;Released.
CONTINUED ABOVE.

USP.AC FORM 175 1-21-37-200

Medical, Neuro-Psychiatrical, Educational, Religious, Social and Employments.
Medical Exam: Syphilis secondary;Physically able to do any work assigned to him;Neuro-Psych:average intelligence;He is a married man the Catholic Religion and has 6th grade education;Admits use of liquor but denies use of drugs;Not much known of early life but it is apparent he has been connected with every known vice & racket prior to conviction in present offense;Was known as "Public Enemy No.One".

NARA

Witnesses were killed

or threatened, so no one would testify against Capone. Although he was arrested and indicted numerous times (see Criminal History left), most charges were dismissed. It took federal investigators months to amass enough financial data to bring federal charges on income tax evasion against him. He had served time in Pennsylvania's Eastern State Penitentiary from May 1929 until March 1930 but in relative comfort. Alcatraz was the top maximum security penitentiary in the federal prison system and far more restrictive.

letters from strangers (filed), and once, boxes of fruit which guards distributed to charity. Everywhere Johnston appeared, in fact, people asked about him. But Johnston could not be swayed; Capone was just a number like everyone else.

In fact he was a typical Alcatraz convict, self-absorbed and quick to lash out. Initially, he worked in the laundry, but at times he proved to be a bully. After a fight with another con, he was transferred to the shower room as an orderly. (Cons derisively called him the "Wop with the mop.")

He had entered a prison population that wasn't always friendly toward him. Alcatraz had *clicks*, prisoner Al Best later wrote. Best, #107, convicted for writing bad checks, wrote that there was the Texas-Oklahoma crowd; the "Machine Gun" Kelly crowd, which included Albert Bates and the legendary Harvey Bailey; the Barker gang, which included Alvin "Ol' Creepy" Karpis and nine or ten other men; the "Frisco" gang with John Paul Chase, a partner of "Baby Face" Nelson who had been a bootlegger in the San Francisco Bay Area; and the soldiers—leftovers from the military prison days—who mostly kept to themselves. There were also members of the "Terrible Touhy" mob, a rival Chicago bootlegging gang. Capone had to bob and weave

his way around convicts who were jealous or attracted to him, guys who had scores to settle or who hoped he could bankroll their escape plan.

He incurred the normal infractions: talking in line, talking at the dining table, spitting, fighting. He was stabbed, but not seriously, by Jimmy "Ice-Box Annie" Lucas in 1936 who was aiming to make a name for himself. But Capone's life would never be the same.

What happens to a man when he is stripped of all vestiges of money and power—his silk ties and custom-made suits, his rigged-up Cadillac, his cash and bodyguards? What happens when he is forced to wear the same ill-fitting clothes as everyone else day in and day out? When he has no money? And worse, when he sits alone in his cell for hours unable to talk?

His decline was slow at first and then steep. On Saturday, February 5, 1938, he put on his Sunday clothes rather than his coveralls, then couldn't find his cell. By then he shuffled like an old man and his speech was slurred—classic symptoms of neurologic syphilis. When the bars closed behind him, he appeared incoherent then lapsed into convulsions that resembled an epileptic seizure. His body became rigid and he bit his tongue. Eventually he stopped seizing and was carried into the

Capone in 1941 with his trademark cigar and his lawyer, Abe Teitelbaum, still acting the part of the celebrity gangster.
AP Wide World Photos

hospital on a stretcher. He drifted into unconsciousness then awoke hours later confused and unable to control his bowels or his bladder. In November, when told that he couldn't go to the yard, he "flew into a rage, kicking the door and cursing everyone. He destroyed his blue uniform and bath robe and . . . kept this up for about one hour."

It has been written that Capone refused treatment for syphilis because he feared needles. That isn't accurate. He refused a spinal tap that would determine if the disease had spread to the brain, which it does in about 10 percent of the cases. But he received several courses of heavy metal injections, such as bismuth and arsenic, while on Alcatraz. And he also permitted doctors to inoculate him with malaria, a startling practice that was thought to raise the body's temperature and destroy the spirochetes. An Alcatraz report, on September 17, 1938, detailed a malarial chill that raised his temperature to 104 degrees and caused another seizure and partial paralysis. Dr. Romney M. Ritchey, chief medical officer, was so frightened that his most famous patient would die that he discontinued treatment.

For the next year until he departed Alcatraz, Capone remained upstairs in the prison's hospital. He suffered

wide mood swings—becoming magnanimous and jovial, and then deflated and childish. He made and unmade his bed at times, and according to Dr. Milton Beacher, he sometimes sang Italian arias.

Capone departed Alcatraz on January 6, 1939, paroled out on November 16, 1939 and moved into his Miami mansion. Although there were glimpses of his former rock-star status—he showed up in photographs dressed in fancy clothes, his ubiquitous cigar clamped between his always smiling lips—they were just flashes. Most of the time he remained at home with Mae, dressed in pajamas, slippers and a robe. His disease degenerated, his moods swings became wilder. Mae, his brother, Ralph, and others helped care for him around the clock.

Just days after his birthday in 1947, he suffered a stroke. While in the hospital he contracted pneumonia. It was the one-two-three punch of a neurological breakdown; first the brain goes, then the lungs and finally the heart gives out. He died of cardiac arrest on Saturday, January 25, 1947. He was 48 years old. And he still owed back taxes.

Welcome to Paradise

"Machine Gun" Kelly 1895–1954

George Francis Barnes, Jr. was a high-school kid whose first crime was to blackmail his father—who was having an affair—for a bigger allowance and unlimited use of the family car.

Daddy should have been a man, maybe apologized to his son, maybe had a man-to-man talk about how his wife, Junior's mother, was not quite who she pretended to be and who filled his head with unrealistic expectations, promising that he was better than others and deserved to live in luxury. Maybe then Senior would have been the moral compass that turned his son's life around.

But Daddy caved. And Junior, the Memphis entrepreneur, used the car to cross Tennessee state lines to buy liquor for his teenage friends. This early successful turn on blackmail and bootlegging had disastrous consequences for the popular kid. It led to a short crime spree that ended in a spectacular kidnapping and a long, slow life sentence spent mostly on Alcatraz.

His mother died when George was a teenager and the cocky kid, who hated his father, was shattered. He left home, got married at 19, had two kids, and took a job with his father-in-law, a man he admired. In fact, he changed his name to George Ramsey Kelly, in honor of his mother and his father-in-law. And for a few years George had it made. But when his father-in-law died, it took the support out of his life. Suddenly he was out of work with a wife and two kids to support. He fell back into bootlegging and he drank; his youngest son later remembered him as a mean drunk.

Kelly was small-time. He lived from deal to deal, flush with cash one moment, broke the next. He loved clothes and cars, and his long absences and wallowing self-pity led to his divorce in 1926. The next year he was in New Mexico state prison for boot-legging. In 1928 he got three more years for bootlegging and was sent to the U.S. penitentiary in Leavenworth, Kansas.

By then he had already met another woman who would finish wrecking his life.

Kathryn "Kit" Kelly (né Cleo Mae Brooks Thorne) was a rakish, narcissistic, double-dealing dame who'd been married three times and quite probably had killed her previous husband. Despite the fact that Charley Thorne was shot between the eyes and had typed his suicide note (he was illiterate), the coroner had ruled it suicide. George was so smitten he probably didn't care; they were both handsome, cheeky, and they drank too much.

Talk about loop de loop. They were both status-seekers who didn't feel alive unless they had new cars or clothes. They lived for the moment, not caring if their actions had consequences for themselves or others. It was Kathryn who bought George his first machine gun, urged him to target shoot and then distributed the bullet casings to others, calling him "the big guy" or "Machine Gun" Kelly. With her urging, Kelly and his Leavenworth pals began pulling bank jobs.

It was exciting—driving around the Midwest robbing banks in new cars. In 1933, sheriffs in cities as far and wide as Tacoma, Ft. Worth, Denver, Oklahoma City, Kansas City and Los Angeles all requested Kelly's mug shots for robberies, although it's doubtful he committed

all of them. Federal laws enacted in 1930 enabled the FBI to track criminals across state lines. But the challenge for police everywhere was poor communications and cars. Gangsters could rob banks and escape into the next state before the cops could crank up their engines. And gangsters had bigger, faster cars than the cops. In fact, George bought cars like candy. He had Cadillac Coupes, Cadillac Sedans; he claimed to have purchased five Fords from the same Ft. Worth dealership. When his son visited him at Alcatraz 15 years later, George's second question was, "Have you seen the new Cadillacs?"

In the summer of 1933, Kathryn and the big guy started talking about kidnapping as a means of grabbing more cash. Kidnapping became a federal offense after Charles Lindbergh's baby had been taken. But Kit and Kelly thought they were smarter than the feds.

The most telling anecdote about Kathryn, in fact, occurred at a party while she was drinking. She began chatting up two men who happened to be Ft. Worth police detectives. Mistakenly thinking there were crooked (why else would they be at the party?) she offered them a piece of the action if they would protect her and Kelly. The detectives declined and later filed a report.

The Kellys were amateurs. Their first victim convinced them that he had no money and they released him but demanded he send $50,000 "or else."

Then Kelly hooked up with Albert Bates, a 41-year-old career criminal whose crimes dated to 1907. At the time he was wanted in eight states mostly for burglaries and escapes. Bates had run away from home at age 15 and had never had a legitimate job. Although he came from a comfortable home, attended Catholic school and had an IQ of 118, he was emotionally unstable, quick tempered and impulsive. Later a prison psychiatrist wrote that at times he was "completely dominated by strong emotions," a trait he shared with many prisoners.

Searching the newspapers for a suitably rich victim, the two criminals happened on a mention of Oklahoma City oilman, Charles F. Urschel. About midnight on Saturday, July 22, 1933, Kelly and Bates burst into the sun porch where Urschel and his wife were playing bridge with another couple. Kelly was armed with his machine gun, Bates a .45 pistol. Suddenly they realized they didn't know what Urschel looked like. "Which one's Urschel?" Kelly demanded. When no one responded, they grabbed both men and shoved them out the door.

After they sorted out who their intended target was, they drove Urschel all night with his eyes blindfolded and his ears covered. During their 14-hour odyssey from Oklahoma City to the North Texas plains, they ran out of gas, switched cars, encountered a rainstorm and got stuck in mud, got lost and actually asked someone, "How do you get to Paradise?" Finally, they arrived at the farm of Kathryn's mother, Ora, and step-father, Robert "Boss" Shannon, near Paradise, Texas where they chained Urschel to the furniture for the next nine days.

Since Charles was abducted in front of witnesses, there was no question of calling the authorities, and the local

"Machine Gun" Kelly (1) on the morning he was arrested. He'd been up all night drinking. Kathryn Kelly (2) in her arrest photo that morning. She insisted on getting dressed in her favorite monkey fur suit for this shot. Albert Bates (3) used a .45 in the Urschel

kidnapping. He served twice on Alcatraz and died there. Ora Shannon (4), Kathryn's mother, who, along with her husband and son, held Urschel captive, also went to prison. "She is very smooth" her prison report stated, "and too polite and proper to be true."

police urged his wife to call a new FBI hotline. Within minutes she was talking to the FBI Director, J. Edgar Hoover. Agents took up residence nearby while the media camped outside. This would be a big national story.

The kidnappers demanded $200,000 and warned the family that any deviation from their instructions would mean his death. Once the money was assembled, as directed, they placed a classified ad in a newspaper about a farm for sale that included a box number, which Kelly used for further instructions.

Back in Paradise, Urschel was the victim no kidnapper wanted. Assured, self-reliant and possessed with an incandescent memory, he quashed his fear and concentrated on details. Under interrogation by agents later, he recalled their voices, the sounds of the barnyard animals, the layout of the three-room shack where he was kept, the unique taste of the well water and the sound of the squeaky pulley used to bring it up. He consciously left fingerprints every time he moved. But his most important clue was a twin-engine airplane that flew overhead.

The airline industry was young; only two airplanes flew overhead each day. After he noticed a pattern, he casually asked the time. Urschel was cordial, making small talk with "Boss" Shannon and his son, Armon, in whose shack

> The Kellys eluded capture for six weeks, much to Hoover's discomfort.

he was housed. Kathryn's mother, Ora, who was later described in prison reports as a "smooth operator," fed him and no doubt he was polite to her. The men talked of hunting and fishing and sometimes Armon played the violin. When another plane flew in the afternoons, Urschel again asked the time. All week long, as he was confined on the Shannon farm, he noted that the airplanes flew twice each day at the same time—except once when a storm hit.

By the week's end, the ransom money was assembled. Ten thousand $20 bills, each with its serial number recorded by FBI agents, were placed in a satchel and delivered in Kansas City. Kelly personally picked up the loot and was identified in mug shots later. After he took out $11,500 for expenses, he and Bates got $94,250 each and split up. Urschel was driven to Norman, Oklahoma, given $10 and dumped unharmed. Kathryn apparently wanted to kill him but Kelly argued against it.

After debriefing Urschel, the FBI contacted airline officials and the U.S. Weather Bureau meteorologists to triangulate the probable location of the farm. Agents on the ground found the Texas hideout as described by Urschel and J. Edgar Hoover ordered up the posse.

That summer, the "Machine Gun" Kelly kidnapping and manhunt was one of the biggest national news stories. Agents raided the farm on August 12—21 days after the kidnapping—and rounded up Kathryn's mother, Ora, her husband, "Boss" Shannon, her son, Armon, and his wife.

Also caught up in the arrest was Harvey Bailey, one of the most renowned criminals of the day. Known as "the king of the heist men," Bailey was a colorful character who later claimed to be involved in a spectacular Lincoln, Nebraska bank robbery that netted $2.6 million and forced the bank into liquidation. (He was never convicted.) Laid up because of an injury after an escape from Kansas State Prison, Bailey had, oops, ransom money in

his pocket.

That same day, Bates was picked up on unrelated charges in Denver, Colorado and he too was carrying $600 of the ransom money. He was quickly returned to Oklahoma.

For six more weeks Kit and Kelly eluded officers, much to the FBI's discomfort. They traveled from Tulsa to Chicago; Kathryn bought a car in Texas; they visited Minneapolis and, eventually, Memphis. They wrote threatening letters to men involved in the case. "Ignorant Charles," they wrote to Urschel, "Just a few lines to let you know that I am getting my plans made to destroy your so-called mansion, and you and your family . . ." They drove six different cars, according to later prison reports, including a "16-cylinder Cadillac." When they heard

Harvey Bailey, "King of the Heist Men"

that Kathryn's mother and step-father had been arrested, Kathryn panicked and began trying to contact authorities—unbeknownst to her husband—to bargain for *his* arrest in exchange for her mother.

At one point, she and Kelly split up—since cops were looking for a couple—and she picked up an out-of-work, hitchhiking couple, Luther and Flossie Arnold, and their 12-year-old daughter, Geraldine. The Arnolds were no match for the beguiling, rich, fast-talking Kit. She bribed Luther to go to the district attorney and offer up her husband in exchange for herself and her mother. The D.A. no doubt smirked, and refused.

Then Kelly circled back and the two of them concocted a new scheme to travel with Geraldine as a front. Kelly dyed his hair yellow, Kathryn donned a wig, but they were disorganized and loose when drinking and Geraldine took it in.

Incredibly, Kathryn then sent the 12-year-old to Texas with her brother-in-law to retrieve some of the buried money. That game plan failed—her brother-in-law was spotted on surveillance and followed. (Later, $73,240 was found buried on the Texas land owned by Kathryn's uncle.) He put Geraldine on a train and wired her father when she would arrive. But Daddy—who wasn't too bright—had already been arrested after bragging that he was on the Kelly payroll. He and the FBI were waiting for

"Machine Gun" Kelly

Kathryn Kelly liked *attention and it didn't matter how she got it. Here she is being led away by authorities after being given a life sentence. She has probably seen George for the last time in their lives.*

Geraldine when she arrived. Later, reporters surrounded the child. "He and Mrs. Kelly bought me pretty clothes," she told them. "He got mad at me only once, when I didn't want him to drink some whiskey."

Geraldine revealed to agents that the Kellys were going to Memphis, and on September 26, 1933, George "Machine Gun" Kelly and Kathryn were captured without incident. Kelly had been up all night drinking. A half dozen gin bottles and ten empty bottles of "Old Log Cabin" bourbon were strewn about the house. He looked defeated, tired. Kathryn, on the other hand, demanded time to dress properly; she wanted to look good for the photo op. The fast part of their lives was finished.

It was the highest profile kidnapping and capture that year, and it practically made J. Edgar Hoover's career. The first trial held in mid-September had already netted numerous guilty verdicts. Now Kelly and Kit would face trial. The media covered all of the high jinks. At one point Kelly passed Urschel as he walked out of the courtroom and drew his finger across his throat. Urschel defiantly stared back at him. In another incident in the hallway, Kathryn slapped an agent who shoved her while she attempted to kiss her father. Kelly tried to intervene but was hit with the butt of a gun.

In all, twenty-one people were sentenced to prison and six of them—Kelly, Kathryn, Albert Bates, Ora, "Boss" Shannon and Harvey Bailey—were sentenced to life terms. "My Pekinese dog would have gotten a life sentence in this court," Kathryn snorted. Arnon turned state's

witness and won a 10-year suspended sentence.

En route to Leavenworth, in October 1933, Kelly bragged that he'd be back with Kathryn by Christmas. But he was just, as cons said, "selling wolf tickets."

Kelly, Bates and Bailey were taken to Leavenworth, but only to be held for transfer to Alcatraz where they would become numbers 117, 137 and 139 respectively. Only Bates knew that it wouldn't be paradise. Earlier in life he had joined the Army and served 15 months at the Army Disciplinary Barracks on Alcatraz for desertion before being dishonorably discharged. It would be a toss up which was worse, the army prison or the federal pen.

Kelly was 39 when he arrived on the Rock, where he would spend the next 17 years.

Prison records don't tell the whole story, but they show what a man is made of. You can gauge his educational level, his maturity, his insight into his predicament. You

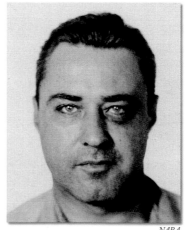

Kelly was convicted on October 12, 1933. Two days later, he got his mug shot at Leavenworth with a black eye.

can see what he's been reduced to and how he reacts. Human beings are remarkably consistent over the course of their lives. In one of his first disciplinary reports, Kelly was caught carrying his prison coveralls to the tailor shop to have them fitted. Ever the narcissist, he wanted to look good even in prison.

He worked on a cell house labor crew the first two years. That meant he seldom left the building. But early in 1936 he began working in Industries, eventually becoming a payroll clerk. His work record was stable, but ques-

tions about his character often cropped up. "He has a 'big shot' complex that is so ingrained that we just take it as a matter of course," one report stated.

His big concern *that first decade* was how many letters he could write and receive from Kathryn who was serving time at Seagoville, Texas and later Alderson, West Virginia. Both prisons had more lenient letter-writing privileges. But Alcatraz ruled, and initially Kelly could receive only one letter a month from his wife. By 1939, he could write and receive two a month. Finally in 1941, seven years after his arrival, he could correspond with her once a week.

But Kelly was still a schemer. In an incredible letter to the U.S. Attorney General in 1936, Kelly asked to be moved to an isolated island to make a meteorological survey of atmospheric conditions. "I could be taken from here secretly," he wrote, "and [be] transported with what supplies I would need . . ." He proposed that this would benefit science and government and suggested that "some kind of arrangement could be made for a boat to stop, say, every year or two, leave supplies and take back what data I had accumulated."

In 1940, he wrote to Urschel. Oil had been discovered near Kelly's land and he wanted to know if Urschel had the "low down" on any land purchases. He also imagined that Urschel was curious about his life and this took up the bulk of his three-page letter. "My cell, made of steel and concrete is always a trifle chilly," he wrote. "My one obsession is the climate of the island. I am constantly bothered with colds." He apologized for his behavior in the courtroom that day, "I was good and mad."

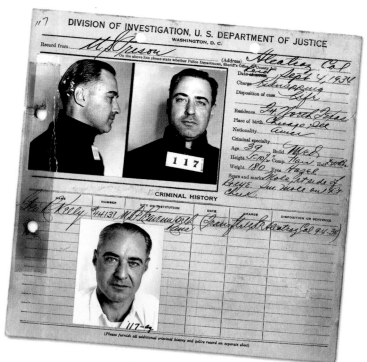

Kelly, left, the taller of the two men whose faces are visible. Next to him is Willie Radkey, AZ# 666, who paroled out of prison and lived to be nearly 100 years old. He returned to Alcatraz several times and identified Kelly in this photograph.

GGNRA/PARC GOGA 19200.280

Kelly was a descriptive writer, "A person in prison can't keep from being haunted by a vision of life as it used to be," he wrote, "when it was real and lovely. At such times I pay with a sense of delicious, overwhelming melancholy, my tribute to life as it once was." But not once in the three-page letter did he apologize for chaining Urschel to a chair for nine days and extracting nearly a quarter of a million dollars from him. Ever the self-involved man, it probably never occurred to him.

Urschel wasn't curious about Kelly's life. But he was curious about the money. Nearly $70,000 had never been recovered. Alcatraz Captain of the Guards, Phil Bergen, once said that Urschel came to the prison several times seeking to intimidate Bates and Kelly into coughing up the cash. Indeed, Urschel wrote "Boss" Shannon and Bates several letters. He visited Bates at Leavenworth. Bates in fact, later pleaded with authorities to stop the contact.

Bates' life on Alcatraz was also tough. He was involved in several strikes, he was written up for talking, was caught with contraband and he fought with other cons. He began to settle down by the mid '40s. But by then he was having heart trouble. In May 1948, he was admitted to the prison hospital. His wife had filed for divorce, and he seemed resigned to death. Just before he died, Kelly was allowed to visit to see if he could "secure information as to where he had hidden the ransom." Alas, even Kelly was unable to dig it out of him. Bates died

July, 1948. He was 55.

By 1941, Kelly began asking for a transfer off the Rock. But it wasn't until late that decade before anyone on Alcatraz even recommended to the Bureau of Prisons in Washington, D.C. that he be moved. Even Harvey Bailey left Alcatraz before Kelly.

He was finally transferred to Leavenworth in 1951. He had matured by then; his hair was gray but he still had his matinee idol looks. He had become a good worker. He was popular, although cons didn't think much of his "Machine Gun" reputation. He still hoped he would one day be free. But he never got out. This photograph below, taken four months before he died, shows the ravages of heart disease. He looks haggard and his face appears bloated. He died in prison in 1954 on his 59th birthday.

In the end, Kelly and Kathryn were a deadly duo whose corrupt characteristics multiplied once they got together. Kelly was a genial, naive opportunist. Kathryn was scheming and mercenary. They exploited their friends, their family and even strangers to meet their needs. Kathryn's mother, Ora, was described as "dominant and selfish," characteristics which probably also described her daughter. The two were bonded. After they both were released from prison in 1958, Kathryn worked in the same home where Ora was confined. Kathryn died in 1985 at the age of 81.

USPLK-44131 -3-25-54

NARA

GGNRA/PARC GOGA–40046.041

Jolene Babyak

Kelly served 17 years, long enough to see Warden Johnston retire and be replaced by Warden Edwin B. Swope, above.

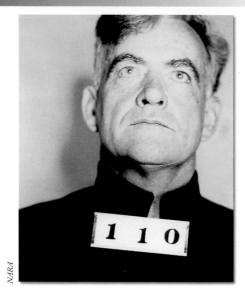

NARA

Roy Gardner was on the same train from Leavenworth as "Machine Gun" Kelly. Although it was Gardner who would have leaned over to see Kelly, and not the other way around, nonetheless Gardner was well known in the western United States. Often called the "last of the great train robbers," he was a thief, an opportunist and a gentleman, but as a train robber he was not so great.

Born in 1884, Gardner was a headstrong kid who quit school by the age of 16, left home and began serving time in a Missouri reform school. He joined, then deserted, the Army. He smuggled arms during the Mexican Revolution, got caught, was nearly executed and escaped.

In 1910, during the busy Christmas shopping season in San Francisco, he grabbed a tray of diamonds and bolted out of a jewelry store with clerks in pursuit. Sometimes opportunity is a poor teacher; he ran headlong into a policeman and got two years in San Quentin state prison.

After prison, he married and had a daughter. But broke and desperate in April 1920, he grabbed a mail pouch full of registered mail from a railroad depot, then robbed a mail messenger at gunpoint in San Diego. He was caught the next day.

He pled guilty, got 25 years and in June 1920, was taken by two armed U.S. Marshals aboard a train to McNeil Island federal prison in Washington. Gardner could talk a good line. As the train neared Portland, he jumped up and exclaimed, "Look at that deer!" When one marshal stood up, Gardner grabbed his gun. Chagrined and humiliated, the two marshals took the handcuffs off Gardner and cuffed themselves. Gardner emptied the gun, and because the marshal was fond of it, returned it to him. He escaped and was on the lam for nearly a year.

He traveled, and found odd jobs, but by May 1921, the lure of easy money led him to hold up a railway postal clerk in Roseville, California. He was caught, given another 25-year sentence, and on June 11, 1921, was again en route to prison on a train with U.S. Marshals.

This time he talked the marshal into unlocking his handcuffs so he could relieve himself. While at the sink he produced a gun hidden beneath his shirt. Once again the marshals and Gardner switched handcuffs and leg irons. Gardner robbed them, probably apologizing as he did, and at 1:20 AM he dropped off the train.

But he was captured days later and finally delivered to the warden.

Not for long, however. Three months later he escaped again. While running, he was shot in the left leg and right thigh. He spent the night hiding in a barn on McNeil Island, dressed his wounds, milked a cow for nourishment, and two nights later swam to Fox Island. He stole a boat, made his way to Portland, then to Sacramento, and by November, he was in Phoenix, Arizona. Meanwhile he wrote about his exploits to a friend who published them in the *San Francisco Bulletin*. On November 15, he held up Herman F. Interlied in yet another mail train robbery. But Interlied got the drop on Gardner and sat on him until the cops came. Gardner later said, "That mail clerk was 100 percent man. And I was a cheap crook."

Gardner would try anything. He pled guilty, took the stand and attempted to appear insane. But it didn't work. He got his third 25-year sentence and was sent to Leavenworth.

A tall, strongly built man, he often used intimidation for great effect. He fought with guards, faked insanity and went on hunger strikes. But it only got him harder time as he was transferred from Leavenworth to Atlanta. There he tried to escape with five other men using a smuggled gun. None of it worked and he began to realize that he was "his own worst enemy."

In 1934, he was one of the few federal prisoners to actually *request* to be sent to Alcatraz to be near his family, and he began to settle down.

In 1938, his sentence was amended to two 25-year concurrent sentences which meant that by end of that year he got out of prison, having served 17 years behind bars.

He wrote a book, ran a "Crime Doesn't Pay" booth at the 1939 Treasure Island Exposition, and then shortly after being given a diagnosis of a terminal illness, he committed suicide by cyanide gas in 1940.

A gentleman to the end he had checked into a hotel, left a note warning the maid not to enter the room and asked reporters not to mention his daughter's name in his obituary because she had not told her in-laws that the infamous Roy Gardner was her father.

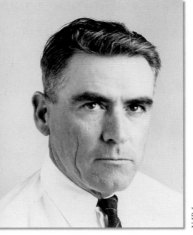

John Paul Chase came to Alcatraz six months after Capone and Kelly. And although some could argue that he remained in prison for 31 years because of one lousy day, as in all similar tales, tragedy and bad decisions led to that day.

Born in 1901, possibly in San Francisco, he left home after his mother died when he was 15. He worked in the railroad yards near Sausalito, now a tony village overlooking San Francisco Bay.

By the 1920s he was operating a rum-running boat with several local hoods. Chase was not much of a criminal; he was arrested only once for public drunkenness. But his bootlegging put him in the company of a man named "Baby Face" Nelson.

Nelson, a psychopath whose real name was Lester Gillis, arrived in the Bay Area after escaping from a train en route to Joliet state prison in February 1932. A self-absorbed, callous kid fascinated with guns, he first went to reform school at age 12 after shooting a gun that injured a boy's face. Eventually his path as a criminal led him to a brazen Chicago robbery, in which he mugged the mayor's wife. She described him as having a "baby face." Nelson was an indiscriminate killer with two outstanding warrants, including one for murder of an FBI agent. He was a wanted man.

Psychopaths are focused and often compelling. Chase was fascinated and hung out with him for the next two years, much to his detriment. Nelson drove, often with his wife at his side, while Chase, armed, sat in back. The two were implicated in numerous crimes including murder and bank

robberies and were the prime suspects in the disappearance of a Reno bank cashier who was to testify against a colleague.

But their big day was November 27,

1934. The three were driving a stolen Ford V-8 from Chicago to Lake Geneva, Wisconsin. In a scene worthy of a crime movie, a car with two agents encountered their car, pulled a U-turn to double check their plates, only to have Nelson make a U-turn, where they met up again. After the cars passed each other, Nelson spun around, got behind the agents' car, and caught up to them as Chase began shooting. Another carload of agents sped up, and after more gunfire, two agents were dead and Nelson was mortally wounded. His body was found the next day in a cemetery, riddled with bullets and wrapped in a blanket.

Chase was caught in California, sent to Alcatraz where he remained for 19 years. He took up painting while on the Rock and produced a nine-panel panorama of the San Francisco Bay. Although he painted the Alcatraz boat on its way to San Francisco, he also drew a fantasy boat, called the *J.P. Chase*, en route to Sausalito. Later, at Leavenworth, he became an expert shoe cobbler, often making shoes for disabled prisoners. He paroled out in 1966, returned to the Bay Area to work as a janitor for a Catholic parish and died in 1972.

The phantom boat, the J.P. Chase, *escaping Alcatraz for Sausalito, where Chase had once lived. Above, Chase's parole card.* NARA

Doc on the Rocks

"Doc" Barker 1899–1939

Something was wrong with the Barker family. Arizona Donnie Clark, called "Arrie," then "Kate," was lionized by J. Edgar Hoover as "Ma" Barker, the "evil genius" behind her four sons' murderous rampages. But only half of that was true.

She married George Barker in the 1890s when she was still a teenager. Little is known about George except that he abandoned the child care to her and appears to be a timorous personality next to Ma's domineering presence. The kids took after her. By the time her four sons were in school, they were wild, disruptive boys with hillbilly haircuts. If they went to school, that is.

By 1910, they were living in Tulsa, Oklahoma. Herman was 16, Lloyd was 14, Arthur was 11 and Freddie was 7. And they all had complaints against them.

Herman, the oldest, was committing residential burglaries, sometimes bringing in Lloyd. He quickly moved into clothing and jewelry store robberies.

Poor Lloyd, the second born, didn't have much of a crime career. He eventually struck out on his own and was caught up in a mail train robbery in 1922 for which he spent 16 years behind bars.

Arthur, Ma's third son, born in 1899, would become the most famous, probably because of his nickname and his Alcatraz connection. He was called "Little Dock" as a kid, then "Dock" and eventually "Doc" Barker, a catchy name that belied his intelligence, which was 20 points below normal. Short, "sleek and oily," Doc was sullen to authority, evasive and nervous. As a kid, he liked to steal and strip cars, especially Ford roadsters, which he did with his younger brother.

Freddie, the baby of the family, should have been the most notorious; he was as mean as a snake. Dominant, wily, impulsive and a showoff, he had four gold teeth in the front of his mouth and was said to be Ma's favorite. Others were stunned by his indiscriminate killing. He stole cars as a kid too, favoring Cadillacs.

The younger three were members of a Tulsa teenage gang, which sometimes had 22 members and were the usual suspects in Tulsa's car thefts, residential burglaries and muggings. As they grew older they began cracking safes and cycling in and out of prisons. Half of them would die by guns, at least three, Doc, Volney Davis and Harry Campbell wound up on Alcatraz.

Ma was often described as overprotective to the point of paranoia. Whenever one went to jail, she screamed at the sheriff until her kid was released. She was suspected of bringing in sulfuric acid and a saw once, to help Doc and 16 others escape a city jail. Another time she confronted the owner of a car stolen by one of her kids and he quickly dropped the charges. Ma was scary.

In time, the two oldest, Herman and Lloyd, began breaking into apartments above jewelry stores at night, boring holes through the floor then lowering themselves down a line. They looted watches, gold chains and diamonds. Small safes were easy to crack in those days, using nitroglycerin or pry tools. But sometimes they simply backed up a truck at the rear entrance and loaded the safes onto the bed. They were unbelievably sloppy however; they were visible to early morning pedestrians and left behind fingerprints. Herman forgot his hat once, which

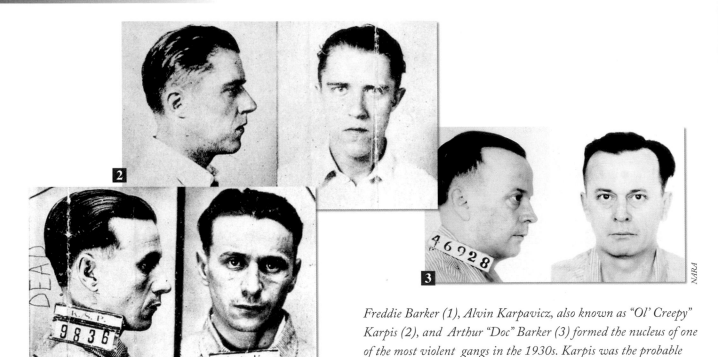

Freddie Barker (1), Alvin Karpavicz, also known as "Ol' Creepy" Karpis (2), and Arthur "Doc" Barker (3) formed the nucleus of one of the most violent gangs in the 1930s. Karpis was the probable organizer. Below, Stillwater, Minnesota state prison, in which Herman Barker served time.

Both courtesy of the Minnesota Historical Society

was traced to him. Eventually he served time in Montana and Minnesota state prisons and was a "walking billboard" of prison tattoos.

"Doc" Barker was the first to be involved in murder. A construction site night watchman was found in 1921 shot in the head and the heart by two different guns. Suspicion immediately fell on Volney Davis who had just quit working there, and bullets at the scene led to the convictions of murder by both Davis and Barker. Both drew prison time in Oklahoma, Barker serving the next 10 years.

By 1927 Freddie, the baby of the family, was also serving a five-to-ten year sentence at Kansas state penitentiary in Lansing for burglary. Then Herman died that year. After escaping from an Arkansas jail and fatally shooting a sheriff in the back, he and another thug were pulled over by two cops for speeding. As Officer Joseph Marshall approached the car window, Herman grabbed him by the throat and shot him in the face. The other man jumped out, shot Officer Frank Bush, then fled. Bush recovered, and as Herman was trying to drive away, Officer Bush shot point blank into the car window.

Witnesses saw the car weave across the street and bump into the curb. Herman, shot in the head, cried out that he couldn't see. He staggered over to an abandoned lot and fell into the weeds. Witnesses heard a "deep, heavy moaning," and then a gunshot blast. Herman had killed himself. He was 33.

There was Ma, all alone in 1927, one son dead and three

in prison.

Freddie heard about his oldest brother's death while in Lansing, but he had a new friend—Alvin Karpavicz. "Karpis" for short, called "Ray" by his friends and known as "Ol' Creepy" because of his startling eyes and slinky gait, he would one day be "Public Enemy No. 1" because of his association with the Barker boys.

It's easy to think of Freddie as an evil, giggling hick who would one day get himself killed. But with Karpis, Freddie got organized. The two heard how to spot the days when big payrolls were carried into banks. They learned how to map an escape route, called a "git," which detailed the back street routes out of town. The two men, along with "Doc" Barker, would form the nucleus of one of the most destructive gangs in the 1930s.

Freddie and Karpis tumbled out of prison in May 1931. Ma had divorced George and was now calling herself Kate. She was literally shacked up near the railroad tracks with a man named Arthur Dunlop, a silver-haired, 65-year-old drunk. One of the Barker boys' girlfriends later called him, "too lazy to work, too scared to steal."

Seven months after the two men left prison they grabbed Ma and Dunlop and fled the state. One of them had killed Sheriff C. Roy Kelly during a robbery in West Plains, Missouri. Wanted posters popped up everywhere, naming Karpis, Freddie, "Old Lady Arrie" and Dunlop for a combined reward of $1,200. The four headed for St. Paul, Minnesota and a casino called the Green Lantern.

St. Paul, Minnesota was a key to understanding the crime spree in the 1930s. It had been a gangster haven since 1900, when a crooked police chief, John J. O'Connor, announced that criminals could "layover" in town without threat of arrest—so long as they didn't commit crimes there. Harry Sawyer's Green Lantern casino was a gangster clearinghouse where criminals met, planned their jobs and solicited help. Another casino owner, suave, smarmy Jack Peifer (who was so inept with a gun that he reportedly shot off the tip of his penis

Ma Barker, in an undated photograph. J. Edgar Hoover portrayed her as the mastermind of the Karpis-Barker gang, but according to Harvey Bailey, "She couldn't plan breakfast."

The Gang's

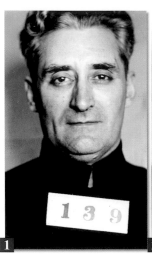

Members at various times of the Karpis–Barker gang who ended up on Alcatraz, Harvey Bailey (1), who robbed a Ft. Scott, Kansas bank with the gang; "Doc" Barker (2), Volney Davis (3), casino owner Harry Sawyer (4) and Elmer Farmer (5). Volney Davis was a childhood friend of the Barker's in Tulsa. He was luckier than they were; he got out of prison and lived to be an old man.

while pulling his Derringer out of his pants) regularly laundered money for the big timers—John Dillinger, Fred Goetz, alias "Shotgun George Ziegler" of the Al Capone mob, members of the "Terrible Touhy" gang and perhaps even "Machine Gun" Kelly. Peifer was a fixer. Both Sawyer and Peifer paid off cops on a weekly basis and were tipped to any raids. And the biggest crooked cop was Detective Tom Brown who would become a rich man on their crimes.

Peifer's casino, the Hollyhocks, was the sparkling showcase that Christmas as fancy cars swept into the snowy Minnesota parking lot. Men in black and ladies in red were ushered inside where formally attired croupiers kept the spirit giddy and warm. Karpis and Barker couldn't believe it. Nearly a quarter of the population was out of work from the Depression, but you couldn't tell here. Ma, Dunlop, Freddie and Karpis took up residence in St. Paul calling themselves the "Anderson" family.

Because criminals flocked to St. Paul, Karpis and Freddie Barker were able to recruit others to their schemes and at times the Karpis-Barker gang used as many as 11 men to pull off some of their crimes. From the spring of 1931 until each man was killed or imprisoned by 1936, they were suspected of being involved in 13 robberies in which 8 people were killed. Two of the victims were women who were about to testify against them. Four were police. They stopped at nothing. In January 1932, Karpis and Barker held the town marshal and a garage attendant hostage in Cam-

bridge, Minnesota, and ransacked the town. By March, they hit a bank in Minneapolis, holding off 28 customers and employees with machine guns and Freddie's loud intimidation. They got $75,000 cash, $6,500 in coins and $185,000 in bonds. In June, they hooked up with Harvey Bailey and robbed a bank in Ft. Scott, Kansas.

They bought cars and gave Ma a fur coat. Dining at the Hollyhocks frequently, they had cash and female attention. Karpis romanced his teenaged girlfriend there. When someone notified the police anticipating the $1,200 reward, Tom Brown tipped them off and the four fled minutes before the raid. They ran out of the house leaving the stove and the lights on. They left behind Ma's fur coat, a camera with undeveloped film inside and a $500 bond from an Iowa bank robbery. But they grabbed the silverware.

On the "git" out of town, Karpis and Freddie mistakenly focused on Dunlop as their snitch. He turned up naked, alongside a Wisconsin lake, with a fatal bullet wound in his head. Then Ma and her two boys rented an eight-room house in a nearby resort community, now calling themselves the "Hunter" family.

By September, when Doc got out of prison and joined Karpis and Freddie, the gang's violence escalated. They robbed a North Dakota bank that month and Freddie pistol-whipped a bank cashier. They grabbed hostages and used them as shields on the running boards of their car, then tossed roofing nails onto the road behind them to deter the cop cars. They were characters in a Holly-

All Here

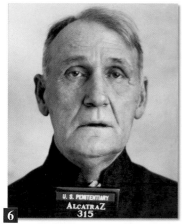

Other members of the gang were Charles "Big Fitz" Fitzgerald (6), Harry Campbell (7), Karpis (8) and Fred Hunter (9). Campbell was another childhood friend of the Barker kids. Both Campbell and Hunter were with Karpis when he was "Public Enemy No. 1." Hunter was arrested with him in New Orleans and in 1943 tried to escape from Alcatraz.

wood movie, these guys.

In a daring, daylight Minneapolis bank robbery that December, they fatally shot two police officers who responded, and minutes later, Freddie impulsively shot an innocent bystander in the head, killing him. The others were shocked, but Freddie argued that the man was too interested in their activities.

They had other problems. Doc drank too much. Even Freddie thought he was unreliable.

Then the kidnappings began.

Jack Peifer called a meeting in the spring of 1933 in which he proposed they kidnap Theodore Hamm, Jr. for a ransom. Everyone was surprised. Hamm was the 38-year-old president of Hamm's Brewery, one of St. Paul's biggest businesses. Peifer explained that the "O'Connor layover" had fallen and a reform-minded police chief had been elected. This kidnapping, which would involve Detective Tom Brown, would be their revenge.

On June 15, at about noon, Doc and Charles "Big Fitz" Fitzgerald accosted Hamm and pushed him into Karpis' car. Taken to Illinois, Hamm was held hostage for nearly two weeks while the family put together $100,000.

This was a big operation involving nine men. Several times cops were close, but the tips were relayed to Detective Tom Brown who promptly warned the kidnappers. And he was paid handsomely for his part. He eventually got a quarter of the haul—$25,000. Peifer got $10,000 just for suggesting the idea. After paying $7,500 to launder the money, $650 to the man who held the hostage, after expenses and a little slush fund for another ailing gangster, the six principal kidnappers—Doc, Freddie, Karpis, Fitzgerald, Fred Goetz and Bryon Bolton—got only $7,800 each. They must have felt gypped.

Six months later, they were at it again. They kidnapped Edward Bremer in January 1934 for $200,000. Bremer was a wealthy banker and son of Adolph Bremer, president of Schmidt Brewery. The gang was so organized they drove with gas cans so they wouldn't have to stop at

The Crooked City Circuit

Corrupt St. Paul, Minnesota politicians gave fugitives sanctuary until 1933, so long as they paid off the cops and didn't commit crimes locally. Chicago, Kansas City, Cleveland, Hot Springs, Arkansas and Reno, Nevada were also on the circuit. Gangs roamed these cities, planning jobs, recruiting and laundering money. The Green Lantern, a St. Paul casino owned by Harry Sawyer (4), was a clearinghouse for criminals and a big reason why many of the biggest 1930s gangs were from the Midwest.

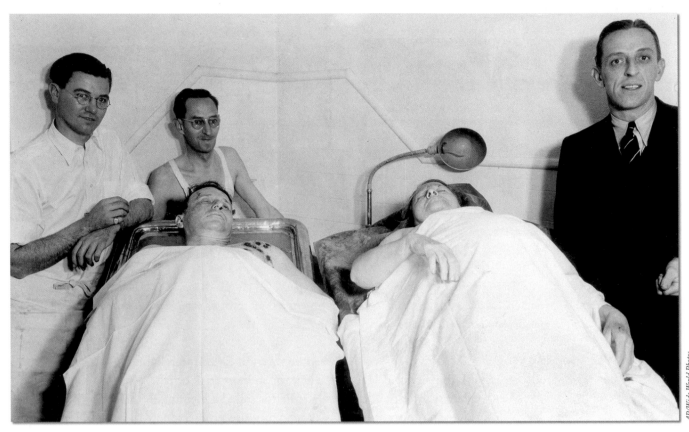

AP/Wide World Photos

Together forever *Freddie and Ma lie dead at the coroner's office after a gun battle with the FBI.*

filling stations. But Doc was sloppy. He pulled alongside a road, emptied the gas into the tank, then tossed the cans. An alert farmer spotted them, scooped them up and, on a hunch, took them to the police.

In the meantime, the ransom was paid, Bremer was released and the gang split up.

It took weeks to identify the prints but finally on March 16, the FBI named the Karpis-Barker gang as the probable kidnappers.

Doc and Volney Davis were already having trouble laundering the money; now they were really hot. They crossed the country from Minneapolis to Reno, a trip that could have taken weeks in those days, but no one wanted anything to do with them. The cash increasingly became a sore spot. Doc carried some of it around in a satchel. Another stash was buried, but water seeped into that and they had to wash and dry the bills individually in a hotel room.

Eleven months after the Bremer kidnapping, the FBI finally got their big break. In December 1934 a district attorney told an agent that his brother was a surgeon who had a patient named Mildred Kuhlman. She just happened to be Doc's girlfriend. Agents found where they

lived, started tailing her, and in January 1935 they arrested "Doc" Barker. While searching his apartment, investigators found a hand-drawn map detailing where Ma and Freddie were holed up in Florida.

The FBI flew down to Lake Weir near Ocala, Florida and staked out the house. On January 16, after sporadic exchanges of gunfire for several hours, agents found both Ma and Freddie dead from gunshot wounds.

FBI Director J. Edgar Hoover was so rattled that they had killed a 60-year-old woman that at a press conference he portrayed her as the gang's mastermind. That began the legend of the "Ma Barker gang." But others who knew her disputed that. The old lady "couldn't plan breakfast," Harvey Bailey once said. And Karpis agreed.

Doc, Volney Davis, Charles Fitzgerald, and casino owner Harry Sawyer were all convicted and sent to Alcatraz. They would soon be joined by Elmer Farmer and Harry Campbell, two other members of the Karpis-Barker gang, and eventually, Karpis and Fred Hunter. Doc and Davis were the first to arrive on October 26, 1935.

By then Alcatraz had been operating about a year as a federal prison, and was still in the tough "silent" years under Warden Johnston. No one knows who started the "escape proof" myth, whether it was the government in response to the killings and escapes in the 1930s, or early cons who got out and wrote books about the dreaded Rock. But of 14 escape attempts in its 29-year history, 10 of them occurred during Johnston's years, as if men were trying to beat back the "escape proof" myth. "Doc" Barker's attempt was number four.

In October 1938 he got into a fight that led to confinement in D block. But that may have been his plan.

D block was the segregation unit, known as "the prison within the prison." But some cons thought it was more desirable; the cells were better ventilated, prisoners had plenty of reading material and they could lay around all day without working. That reasoning appealed to Barker. He had told officers he'd joined a 1937 strike not because of an ideal but because "he had nothin' to lose, wanted nothin' and just quit."

D block looked like A block looks today. The flat, strap bars from the military-prison era had not been replaced by the more modern, round, tool-proof bars in B and C blocks. There was not enough money during the Depression and authorities hoped that cons would overlook that weakness. They didn't. Despite that, no floor officer was assigned to D block either, as in later years, but officers periodically walked in to check on the cons. And the gun gallery officer—locked in a cage that ran the width of the building along the wall from A block into D—was engaged every evening with the dinner transfer in and out of the dining hall. That meant that for nearly an hour-and-a-half every night the segregated cons were virtually unsupervised. It was a monumental oversight, one that officers complained about to higher ups and only too gladly told FBI investigators about later.

Prisoner Dale Stamphill claimed he smuggled in saws and files while working in the cell house. Serving life for kidnapping after an escape attempt from Oklahoma State Prison, Stamphill would one day get out of prison and live in Kansas City. Some of the saws were so tiny, he said, that they were glued to harmonicas for easy smuggling.

William "Ty" Martin, on a 25-year sentence for an armed postal robbery, said that their cell bars had been broken a month or more. Then for an hour each night, while one of them acted as a lookout, several climbed out their cells and worked on the window bars, using a homemade tool they called a "screw jack."

On Friday, January 13, after the 3:00 AM count, Doc, Henry Young, Rufus McCain, "Ty" Martin and Dale Stamphill crawled out of their cells, loosened the window bars and climbed out of the highest custody prison

AP/Wide World Photos

Haunted by death *Agents found a hand drawn map to Ma and Freddie's hideout in "Doc" Barker's Chicago residence after arresting him, above, in January 1935.*

Although mostly photographed on bright, sunny days, Alcatraz was often veiled in a dense fog.

in the nation. The five scrambled down the cliffs on the San Francisco side of the island. When they got to the shore, they stripped and used their clothing to tie together planks of driftwood and an old wooden chair. It was January—they were naked and standing at the cold and windy shore.

At 3:35, an officer discovered one man missing. He quickly telephoned Warden Johnston. By 3:42 officers knew that five men were missing. The escape siren pierced the night air.

About 25 families lived on the island in those days and they were immediately awakened. Johnston worried that cons would take a family member hostage. He dispatched guards to search the family compound, then down to the beaches. The San Francisco Police and the Coast Guard were notified. Guards boarded the island's boat along the north side of the island, and began circling, training a searchlight along the shore.

Young, Martin and McCain, all naked except for their socks, were quickly surrounded by officers, gave up and were escorted back to the cell house.

> ## Doc Barker's death on Alcatraz made them both famous

Stamphill and Barker were along what's now known as "Barker Beach," a little cove on the San Francisco side of the island. Stamphill later said they were trying to swim away, but the tides kept pushing them back. When the boat's searchlight came near them, they hid. Then they tried to make a run for the bay. Officers shouted and when they didn't stop, opened fire with a .45 automatic and a Thompson submachine gun. Stamphill was shot in the legs and immediately incapacitated. Barker was shot in the head. He spoke a few minutes, Stamphill said, then lapsed into semiconsciousness.

Guards loaded the wounded men into a dinghy and dragged it behind the larger boat. Stamphill was still bitter about it years later; he was convinced they were trying to kill him with the exhaust fumes.

Barker was taken to the hospital at 5:15 AM. A bullet had penetrated his leg and broken his thigh bone. He was bleeding profusely. Another bullet had entered his head just below his right ear, passing behind his right eye, which had ruptured and collapsed. His face was swelling and he was bleeding from the nose and ear. He was cold,

CLINICAL RECORD

PROGRESS AND TREATMENT RECORD

Medication	Diet	Daily Notes

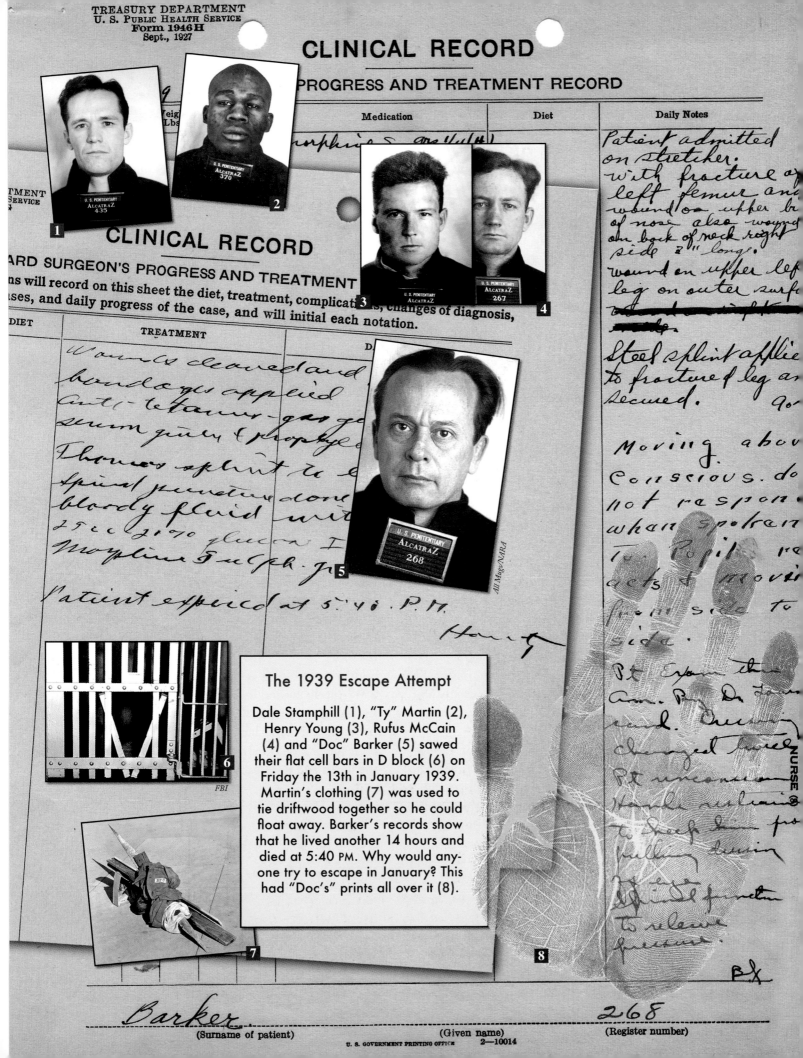

CLINICAL RECORD

...ARD SURGEON'S PROGRESS AND TREATMENT
...ns will record on this sheet the diet, treatment, complicati...s, changes of diagnosis,
...ses, and daily progress of the case, and will initial each notation.

The 1939 Escape Attempt

Dale Stamphill (1), "Ty" Martin (2), Henry Young (3), Rufus McCain (4) and "Doc" Barker (5) sawed their flat cell bars in D block (6) on Friday the 13th in January 1939. Martin's clothing (7) was used to tie driftwood together so he could float away. Barker's records show that he lived another 14 hours and died at 5:40 PM. Why would any-one try to escape in January? This had "Doc's" prints all over it (8).

FBI

All Mugs/NARA

Barker _____ 268

(Surname of patient)   (Given name)   (Register number)

U. S. GOVERNMENT PRINTING OFFICE   2—10014

Henry Young was completely unknown when he arrived on Alcatraz in 1935. The 23-year-old who was serving a 20-year sentence for armed bank robbery, was so inept as a criminal that he got caught because his getaway car had a flat tire. He had already served time in Washington and Montana state prisons and was considered shrewd but emotionally unstable. When he departed Alcatraz 13 years later, Young had racked up more than 30 disciplinary reports including assaults, arson, flooding his cell, attempted escape, attempted murder and finally murder.

He tried to escape in 1939 with "Doc" Barker, Rufus McCain and the others. Then in December 1940 Young stabbed McCain to death for reasons that are unclear. Some thought it was a lovers' quarrel.

Young was never famous. It was the trial and a 1995 movie "inspired" by the trial that made him well known.

The 1941 trial was marked by defense attorney shenanigans that wouldn't be permitted today. Leading questions, a parade of convicts who testified to guard brutality, statements that a "congressional investigation" of Alcatraz was "already underway," and revelations by defense attorneys of a plot (thwarted by them) involving cons killing courtroom participants were the daily fare.

The core of the defense was that Young was in a "psychological coma" from years of solitary confinement and guard brutality, and that he had been placed in the "lower prison" where he went crazy.

Also known as the "Spanish dungeon" although Spain had never occupied Alcatraz, the lower prison was an area behind the shower room wall that had been part of an earlier army building called the Citadel. During the years when the army occupied Alcatraz, disciplined convicts were sometimes held there in rooms that had bars. Even during the early federal prison years, some men were placed there (see photo #5). Most cons, however, knew it only by rumor. When the old army prison became a federal penitentiary in 1934, the first 32 men were army convicts thus insuring that stories of a "Spanish dungeon" exist until today. Warden Johnston testified at Young's trial that the lower prison cells were dismantled in 1938. Captain Phil Bergen, who

U. S. PENITENTIARY
ALCATRAZ

NARA

arrived on Alcatraz in late 1939, also said they were no longer in use when he arrived. It's unclear from Young's record exactly where he was confined after the escape attempt and later after the murder. But he was living in the main population when he actually killed McCain, thus he was not in solitary for three consecutive years.

Nonetheless, the-prison-made-me-do-it defense worked. The jury convicted Young of involuntary manslaughter and gave him a sentence of only three years for McCain's murder. Prisoners who liked McCain were livid.

Young became increasingly unstable as time wore on. After the trial he became religious and confessed to a murder *no one knew about*. He confessed in a letter to Washington authorities and in 1945 he was convicted of killing William Buerig.

Then, in the late '40s he began exhibiting schizophrenic characteristics, such as standing in unusual positions for hours. Prison authorities were unsure if he was faking it or was genuinely mentally ill.

He was transferred in '48 to the federal prison hospital in Springfield, Missouri. After observation he was diagnosed as a paranoid schizophrenic (an organic brain malfunction). He had a "well integrated delusional system" involving psychiatrists, Jesuit priests and the subjugation of the human race.

Young paroled out of federal prison in 1954, but went to Walla Walla, Washington where he served another 18 years for the first murder. He was released in 1972 and disappeared the following year.

In the movie, *Murder in the First*, film critic Roger Ebert wrote that the courtroom furniture was the best part of the movie. Young was depicted as a 17-year-old sent to Alcatraz for stealing five bucks to feed his starving sister, went crazy because of his confinement, killed McCain and finally was found dead in his cell on Alcatraz. "Eventually we stop believing in the story," Ebert wrote, "then we stop caring, and then we start admiring that great furniture."

The Alcatraz furniture refinishing factory.

GGNRA/PARC GOGA-3262

1

2

William Long, Jr.

4

NARA - Wash. D.C.

3

Jolene Babyak

5

GGNRA/PARC GOGA 18352.057

Confinement On Alcatraz

Alcatraz had one cell house where most prisoners were held in B and C cell blocks (1 & 2). Some were placed for punishment in the D block segregation wing (3). A few—Al Capone, "Doc" Barker, "Waxy" Gordon and Robert "The Birdman"Stroud—lived or died upstairs in the hospital (4). Some early cons, perhaps Henry Young, may have been placed in the basement Citadel rooms (5). But the bars were taken out in 1938.

The Longest Yard

"Ol' Creepy" Karpis   1909–1979

When Alvin Karpavicz was a little kid, adults made him nervous and his hands would shake. He had that tic all his life and it would show up in annual classification meetings, the dreaded hearings at which top Alcatraz administrators interviewed prisoners and reviewed their behavior and attitude. Tough meetings for anyone, tougher still for "Karpis" who was on Alcatraz longer than any other con.

His short family history was well known. Born on August 10, 1909, Alvin immigrated with his family from Canada to the United States when he was six. By age 12 he was living with an older, married sister in Topeka, Kansas. She was said to be "bitter towards officials and shares his feelings of oppression." The rest can be guessed. His parents were strict—or mean. He was stubborn and remote, and much of his resentment centered around school.

His parents forced him to go. But he never liked crowds, nor did he do well on tests. He would encounter a problem he couldn't solve and stare out the window, drumming his pencil on his desk. He felt like flinging the paper and stalking out but that wasn't his style. He stopped going after the eighth grade. By then he'd already broken into houses to steal money because he loved having cash and didn't care how he got it. But by 1926, when he was fifteen and a half, he landed a *ten*-year sentence for burglary. His mug shot at the State Industrial School for Boys in Hutchinson, Kansas shows a creepy teenager with swept over hair and angry eyes.

Perhaps because of the hairdo and his eyes, and because he walked on his toes, one of his friends called him that

and he eventually became known as "Ol' Creepy" Karpis. But not to his face.

At 18 he escaped, managing to elude police for a year. When he was caught in March 1930, he was old enough to enter Kansas state penitentiary where he remained until June 1931, serving a total of four years and three months.

Think of it; from age 15 until he was nearly 22—important learning years for anyone—Karpis was warehoused with other teenaged criminals or on the run from cops. Whatever moral training he may have received early in life quickly eroded. His only skill was stealing and running. Worse, he was an ex-con paroled at the onset of a 10-year economic depression. And like many cons, he was bitter and self-absorbed. Later he was quoted saying "he cannot see anything wrong about robbing a bank or kidnapping a person, or killing anybody who interferes." If he'd been a bit smarter he could have turned his life around. Instead, while in prison he met Freddie Barker.

With his four gold teeth and hot personality, Freddie was the opposite of Karpis, the taciturn, calculating lion. Freddie could see Karpis was smart and well-organized. Karpis probably found Ma Barker's youngest son entertaining, and, given Freddie's proclivity for violence, handy to have around. And Karpis was neither as dumb nor as crazy as Freddie, giving him an edge.

But Karpis was only fooling himself. Doing business with Freddie was a two-and-a-half year high followed by three years on the run as the FBI's "Public Enemy No. 1" and 30 more years behind bars, nearly 26 of them on Alcatraz. Seven months after he and Freddie got out

A Canadian served the

1

8 0 0 8

2

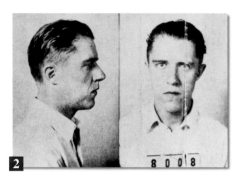

49368

3

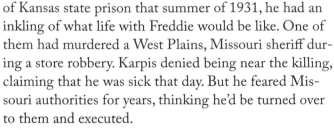

of Kansas state prison that summer of 1931, he had an inkling of what life with Freddie would be like. One of them had murdered a West Plains, Missouri sheriff during a store robbery. Karpis denied being near the killing, claiming that he was sick that day. But he feared Missouri authorities for years, thinking he'd be turned over to them and executed.

And for the next few years, while everyone else fretted about putting food on the table, the Karpis-Barker gang roamed the Midwest, robbing banks, killing witnesses and living lavishly. One problem with crime, however, is the company you keep. Business with Freddie also included "Doc" Barker and Ma, one dim-witted, the other mentally disturbed, and through the years many other criminals, their wives, lovers and kids.

No fewer than 11 men were involved in the Theodore Hamm and Edward Bremer kidnappings in '33 and '34—and all of them had girlfriends. Among them were police detective Tom Brown and two casino owners, Harry Sawyer and Jack Peifer—men with power and money with which to bargain. When one fell, he would bargain, giving up everyone for his safe passage. Those kidnappings were two of the most sensational events in the early 1930s. Only the Lindbergh baby kidnapping, the St. Valentine's Day massacre, the Kansas City Union Station massacre and Kelly's Urschel kidnapping were as notorious. In fact, Karpis was shocked to discover while they held Bremer, that his father, Adolph, was a

"Ol' Creepy" Karpis was one of 13 Canadians to serve time on Alcatraz. At age 15 (1) while at a Kansas reformatory; his 1931 wanted mug shot (2); his 1936 Leavenworth photo (3); at Alcatraz when he arrived in 1936 as #325 (4); updated Alcatraz mugshots, in 1951 (5) and in 1956 (6). In February 1958, Karpis was

U. S. PENITENTIARY
ALCATRAZ
325

4

5

U. S. PENITENTIARY
ALCATRAZ
325
12 11 56

6

longest term on Alcatraz

big contributor to Franklin D. Roosevelt's presidential campaign. Roosevelt reportedly mentioned the kidnapping in one of his weekly radio addresses. Karpis was relieved that they got the money and whole thing was accomplished without killing him. But he must have known that it was only a matter of time.

Nonetheless, Karpis was practical and cagey. When Doc's prints on the gas can were identified and the FBI named the Karpis-Barker gang as the probable kidnappers in March 1934, he sought out a surgeon who could alter his fingerprints.

He found "Doc" Moran, a drunk with a medical degree. Moran had served time and was known among the St. Paul crowd. After dinner one night, Karpis and Doc went to his office. Moran wrapped Doc's knuckles with rubber bands, used a topical anesthetic, then injected each finger with cocaine. "Just like a pencil sharpener" Karpis thought, Moran carved the soft center of Doc's fingers. Later he gave his patient a shot of morphine and a stiff drink. Then Moran started on Karpis, but first he wanted to make some incisions on Karpis' face.

The two men were in and out of consciousness for three days. They showed up at Ma's with their hands wrapped in bandages and Karpis' face swollen. Jeesh, she got hysterical. "Shotgun George Ziegler" Goetz had been gunned down in Chicago and she thought they'd been shot up. They let her wind down, no doubt gave her money and left her behind, Karpis fearing that she

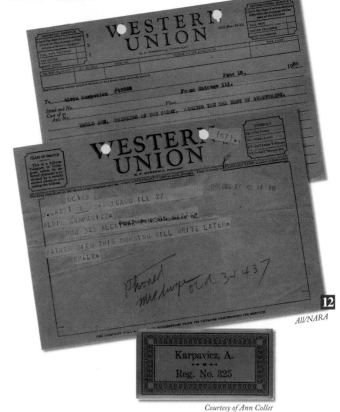

All/NARA

Karpavicz, A.
★ ★ ★ ★
Reg. No. 325

Courtesy of Ann Collet

transferred to Leavenworth (7) but returned to Alcatraz in October (8); finally at McNeil Island in 1962 (9) and in 1969 just before he paroled out (10). Karpis' mangled right thumb print (11) after "surgery." A lifetime behind bars meant that he received news of his father's death via telegram. Karpis' cell card (12). NARA

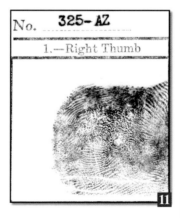

No. 325-AZ
1.—Right Thumb

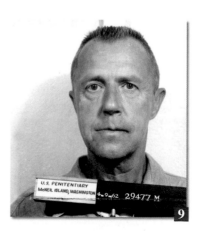

39

Karpis, in the straw hat, handcuffed to Edmund Bartholomey. Bartholomey was a former postmaster who held Theodore Hamm captive in his Illinois home. He got $650 for the job and six years in prison.

would slow them down. They left town.

Ma was the least of their problems. Handling $200,000—in effect, 10,000 twenty-dollar bills—was a panicky proposition. Scads of money got noticed in the third year of the Depression. And such a large sum took up space and caused tension. At times they carried it around in a satchel. They buried some of it, but water seeped in and they had to wash and hang the bills all over their hotel room. Then Moran volunteered to help move it. Ecstatic, Doc brought over $10,000 and agreed to pay him 6 1/4 percent. Moran reportedly got drunk in his hotel while his contacts fanned out to exchange the loot for clean, untraceable money. When he accomplished that, Doc handed him another $20,000. But an alert bank teller identified a serial number on a watch list and one of Moran's men was arrested. Since the stakes were now higher, Moran demanded a bigger percentage, and worse, he began bragging that he worked with the gang. According to Karpis, Freddie and Doc "shot him in the face" then buried him somewhere in Michigan. His body was

never found.

While out on the lam in 1934, Karpis took a legitimate security job in a Cleveland, Ohio casino. He moved there with his pregnant, teenaged girlfriend, Delores Delaney. He liked it; he got to dress up and hang out with gamblers and he was far away from his criminal friends.

But like a live virus in a hot room, they trailed him up there—Freddie and his girlfriend, Harry Sawyer, his wife and their five-year-old adopted daughter. Then Volney Davis showed up demanding his cut of the money. Karpis, chewing his gum loudly and vigorously, tried to keep everyone calm.

Eventually, the gang got a man named "Cash" MacDonald to take $66,000 to Cuba for a 15 percent cut. He was unhappy when they handed him a wad of damp bills.

Karpis had a right to be nervous. The girlfriends were especially troubling. Not too bright, bored and confined to hotel rooms, three of them went out on the town one day in the fall of 1934. They took along Gladys' five-year-old kid, and got so drunk they were arrested. A police matron cornered the little girl and questioned her. That led to a car with a .38 calibre pistol, and then to an apartment with a "gat" in it.

Freddie burst into Karpis' apartment in a panic. Everyone split up again. Doc went back to Chicago, Freddie picked up Ma and headed to Florida. Karpis and Delaney also went south to Cuba.

That January, in 1935, a tip led FBI agents to Doc's girlfriend, which resulted in his arrest. They found the hand-drawn map that led to Ma and Freddie's deaths days later in Florida. Soon Bryan Bolton was arrested. Tired and wanting to deal, he laid out the details of the Hamm and Bremer kidnappings and became the star witness. Volney Davis was arrested, then Harry Sawyer and "Big Fitz" Fitzgerald and Bill Weaver. Just like dominoes.

Agents were sometimes only six to twelve hours behind Karpis but he was able to elude them until April 1936. By then he had abandoned his pregnant girlfriend. (She gave birth to his only son, and served time for harboring a fugitive.)

"Ol' Creepy" was finally nailed in New Orleans. J. Edgar Hoover—still smarting from Senate accusations that he had never arrested anyone, and worse, that his lifestyle hinted at homosexuality—announced with great fanfare that he had personally captured Karpis. Hoover told the story with relish all of his life. Karpis scoffed. Agents surrounded him, he said, then Hoover stepped around a corner to cuff him. Later news accounts stated that no one had brought handcuffs, so they had to use a necktie.

Karpis was tried in May for the Hamm kidnapping and sentenced to life for conspiracy to kidnap. He was in Leavenworth penitentiary by July 29th and on Alcatraz by August 8, 1936, becoming #325. His 27th birthday was two days later.

Karpis had plenty of friends on Alcatraz: Doc, Volney Davis, Charley Fitzgerald, Harvey Bailey, Harry Sawyer, Elmer Farmer and Harry Campbell were all there. Alcatraz opened for these kind of men. Campbell had been involved in several crimes with Karpis, notably a short-lived kidnapping of a doctor whose car they needed. And those were just the guys in the gang. Of course, the great Alphonse Capone was there. Kelly. Charley Berta and Tom Underwood were there—two men who'd gotten guns and dynamite and blasted their way out of Leavenworth in 1931. Harmon Waley was there; he had kidnapped the nine-year-old Weyerhaeuser kid for money and put him in a hole in the ground for days. Who wasn't

Gunning for Karpis *J. Edgar Hoover, above in an FBI publicity photograph, had his own reputation at stake. He claimed to have personally cuffed Karpis in New Orleans, but Karpis told a different tale.*

AP/Wide World Photos

there? Jack Peifer—who was also convicted but who had vowed to never serve time and had swallowed poison just after sentencing and died.

They were all so busy shaking hands and telling stories that no one even noticed the time passing. But life would never be the same for any of them.

Karpis was quiet, polite and cooperative during his early intake meetings, but described as "cold, calculating, indifferent" and "stubbornly self-righteous." Authorities felt that underneath the superficiality was an "unconstitutional psychopath."

And he acted unconcerned. He had eleven disciplinary reports from 1936 until 1945, three of them involving homemade alcohol. He got into fights with other prisoners (including one with Volney Davis) and once hid a knife in his mattress. Several times he acted as a spokes-

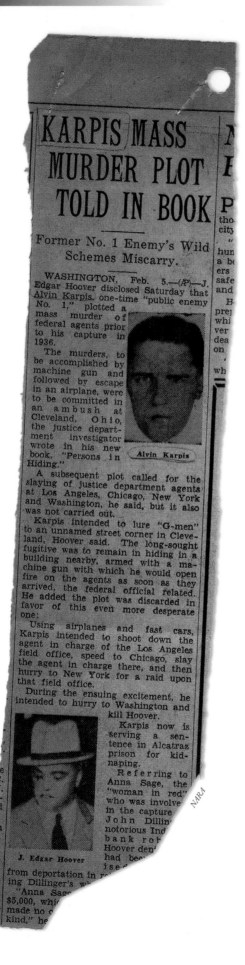

KARPIS MASS MURDER PLOT TOLD IN BOOK

Former No. 1 Enemy's Wild Schemes Miscarry.

WASHINGTON, Feb. 5.—(AP)—J. Edgar Hoover disclosed Saturday that Alvin Karpis, one-time "public enemy No. 1," plotted a mass murder of federal agents prior to his capture in 1936.

The murders, to be accomplished by machine gun and followed by escape in an airplane, were to be committed in an ambush at Cleveland, Ohio, the justice department investigator wrote in his new book, "Persons in Hiding."

A subsequent plot called for the slaying of justice department agents at Los Angeles, Chicago, New York and Washington, he said, but it also was not carried out.

Karpis intended to lure "G-men" to an unnamed street corner in Cleveland, Hoover said. The long-sought fugitive was to remain in hiding in a building nearby, armed with a machine gun with which he would open fire on the agents as soon as they arrived, the federal official related. He added the plot was discarded in favor of this even more desperate one:

Using airplanes and fast cars, Karpis intended to shoot down the agent in charge of the Los Angeles field office, speed to Chicago, slay the agent in charge there, and then hurry to New York for a raid upon that field office.

During the ensuing excitement, he intended to hurry to Washington and kill Hoover.

Karpis now is serving a sentence in Alcatraz prison for kidnaping.

Referring to Anna Sage, the "woman in red" who was involved in the capture John Dilling notorious Ind bank rob Hoover den had bee ise

from deportation in r ing Dillinger's w

"Anna Sag $5,000, whi made no kind,"

Alvin Karpis

J. Edgar Hoover

Paul J. Madigan, above, with his wife Madeline, was the third warden of Alcatraz. Karpis served under all four wardens.

man for inmate grievances, a move that would earn him a label for acting like a "big shot." (Even Morton Sobell, an atypical con who served on Alcatraz for conspiracy to commit espionage, thought it was a stupid move for such a seasoned con. But Karpis, like a lot of cons, seemed unable to override his own tendencies.) By 1945, however, Karpis began to settle down, bringing the same control to his life in prison that he had practiced as a criminal.

Assigned to the kitchen, he became the dessert cook and his behavior improved dramatically. "One of the best workers," a 1949 classification report stated. He studied books on the latest developments in baking. He spent "extra time preparing special ice cream dishes and tasty desserts and [took] great interest in planning inexpensive tidbits on Sundays and holidays." Karpis was so conscientious that he foiled an attempt by someone to sabotage the fruit cake. "Exact details of this incident were not made public," it was reported (and we are sadder for it) but it was felt that his welfare might be in jeopardy if other cons knew. At the classification meeting that year he was awarded a lump sum of $25. It would take another 16 years, but the man who had once commanded hundreds of thousands of dollars in ransoms was now beginning to build the paper trail that would lead him out of prison.

All was not perfect, however. He became "depressed and pouty" over small changes and seldom went to the yard, both indications of a rigid, fearful personality. And when a culinary supervisor initiated new rules in 1952, which curtailed extra food and privileges by kitchen workers, Karpis chose to remain in D block for a year rather than submit to the new rules. After he got out of segregation he never returned to the kitchen crew.

His actions also lost him a recommendation for a transfer off Alcatraz and he was labeled an "agitator."

Instead, when he got out of D block in 1953 he took a job in Industries. When Arthur M. Dollison arrived in October 1953 as an administrator in Industries, Karpis was already working there.

"Karpis was a pleasant surprise," he said years later, "very eager to learn. Tried hard." Dollison said he was easy to talk to, but that was typical and one of the dangers of Alcatraz. "Karpis developed an innocent-looking expression, which he turned on for the staff," he said. "He raised his eyebrows, broke into a wide smile and tried to wipe his face of any meanness. But the result was startling. He couldn't do anything about his eyes."

GGNRA/PARC GOGA-19200.340

The prison's recreation yard, where men could play baseball, handball, checkers, chess and card games using dominoes. Some seldom went to the yard, others never missed a day, rain or shine. For a time Karpis avoided the yard.

There's a regret in seeing a great lion tamed. And yet, once he has killed you can't let him roam. As the years wore on, Karpis grew more docile and his reports grew more complimentary. If he was putting on an act, he had perfected it. By February 1958—after 22 years on the Rock—he was finally transferred to Leavenworth, a lesser custody prison. That also meant that he could one day be paroled, because prisoners usually had to transfer out of Alcatraz before being considered for parole.

But he didn't last at Leavenworth. He was suspected of causing unrest "in an indirect manner," and sent back to Alcatraz in October. Poor "Ol' Creepy"—he was now nearly 50—couldn't help but get others to resist while he chose to speak up. Nonetheless, he accepted his return without rancor and sublimely expressed the hope that he would be given another chance to transfer to a lesser custody prison.

He was reassigned to prison Industries where he again proved to be an excellent worker. A "mature, polite and soft-spoken man," one report called him. Then his June 1960 wrap-up concluded with a remarkable comment, given that this was Alcatraz. "The committee was quite impressed with this man's apparent sincerity and on the basis of his demonstrated efforts . . . the committee recommends that he be given another trial at Leavenworth."

Washington D.C. did not agree, however. It was the Bureau of Prisons director who made transfers on and off

the island prison, and Karpis would remain another year and a half. At one point he wrote a poignant letter asking for a job transfer to the island's dock, noting that even Volney Davis had already been paroled. Then he wrote, "In closing I wish to stress that this letter is solely for the purpose of clarification as regards my thoughts and should in no way be misconstrued as a letter of whining and crying over being sent back here for nothing. . ." He was finally transferred off the Rock in April 1962. He had spent 26 years on Alcatraz, nearly as many years as the federal prison was open. Thus, it was a Canadian who served the longest time in America's most famous prison.

He was transferred to McNeil Island, Washington where his behavior was exemplary. He never asked for special treatment and was never observed expressing bitterness. By 1964 he was in the honor dormitory where he could watch television for the first time. Karpis was taught how to drive a car with automatic transmission, incredibly becoming a night driver for the motor pool.

Karpis was probably not a psychopath. It doesn't appear he was ever tested. But psychiatric professionals believe that psychopaths can't be turned around, that they remain cold, remorseless and indifferent all of their lives because it's embedded in their personality. And Karpis had genuinely become a model prisoner, a man who seemed to relish his good behavior and the rewards that it brought. He had turned his life around—35 years

The south side of Alcatraz showing prisoners walking along the fence from jobs in the Industries building up the stairs on the hill into the prison's recreation yard while the tower officer watches from his catwalk. Karpis saw this view five days a week for almost ten years.

too late, perhaps, and much too late for anyone he might have killed or inconvenienced through kidnapping and extortion.

It would be so neat and tidy to assume that all long-term, violent criminals like Karpis suffer from mental illness. But many neurological, behavioral and situational challenges exist in families which sometimes combine to elicit criminal behavior. Abuse, abandonment, addiction, mental illness or personality disorders are often evident.

But when you review his characteristics over the course of his life—his early defiant behavior, his impulsiveness and organization, his need to get away from the crowd, his tiptoeing around and "creepy" eyes, his obsessive interest in making desserts, his improvement over time in a severely restrictive environment—it's tempting to think that he actually might have had a neurological problem. Toe walking, for example, may be a result of severe anxiety, called "tendon guard reflex" and is sometimes indicative of high functioning autism, or Asperger's Syndrome—which, of course, were undiagnosed in those days. Such symptoms could have worsened in the chaos of early reform school, state prisons and the Great Depression, but lessened in

the restrictive life on Alcatraz.

In one of the most remarkable sentences ever seen in a prison report it was written: "Karpis is part of an era of our society, and it is believed his reckless, antisocial tendencies are as defunct as the conditions that surrounded him in the Prohibition Days. Therefore, we recommend his parole." It was astonishing, given his "Public Enemy" status, that anyone ever considered him good enough for parole and certainly a tribute to his turnaround.

He was paroled in January 1969 and deported to Canada. He reconnected with his only son, wrote a book, *On the Rock*, and taped his memories. He proved to be generally honest and his tapes provided one of the only first-person accounts from that era. Then, in August 1979, just after his 70th birthday, while on vacation in Spain, he killed himself, perhaps accidentally, by mixing alcohol with sleeping pills. He died quietly, in his sleep, just as he had lived most of his life.

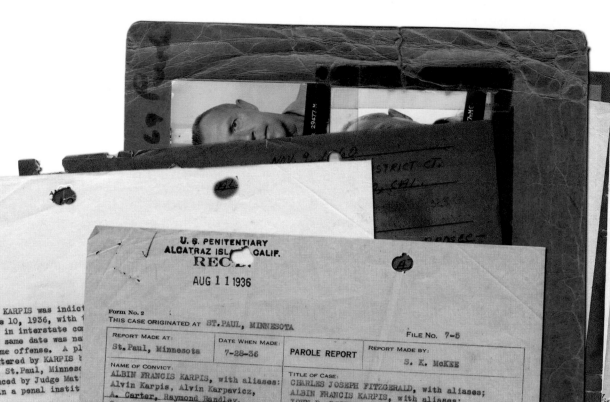

KARPIS was indict_
on June 10, 1936, with _
person in interstate co_
on the same date was na_
the same offense. A pl_
was entered by KARPIS t_
Court, St.Paul, Minneso_
sentenced by Judge Mat_
life in a penal instit_

This crime is _
It is also to be state_
after this kidnaping, _
of her son was partly _

The criminal h_
arrest record, which _
to Agents that he wa_
at St.Paul, Minnesot_
was collected. He i_
Kelley of West Plain_
to Agents by crimina_
crimes:

Murder of A. _
Wisconsin, o_

Robbery of _
along with _
Larry DeVol_

Robbery of _
July 26, 1_
Doyle, and _

Murder of _
Oklahoma, _

Robbery o_
on Decembe_
Doc Barke_
two polic_
getaway; _

U. S. PENITENTIARY
ALCATRAZ ISL___ CALIF.
REC___

AUG 1 1 1936

Form No. 2
THIS CASE ORIGINATED AT ST.PAUL, MINNESOTA

FILE No. 7-5

REPORT MADE AT:	DATE WHEN MADE:	PAROLE REPORT	REPORT MADE BY:
St.Paul, Minnesota	7-28-36		S. K. McKEE

NAME OF CONVICT:
ALBIN FRANCIS KARPIS, with aliases:
Alvin Karpis, Alvin Karpavicz,
A. Carter, Raymond Handley,
George Haller, Alvin Korpis,
A. Korpis, Earl Peel, Alvin Kapis,
George Dunn, R. E. Hamilton,
Ray Hunter, Ray Karpis, E.L.Burns,
Earl Lyman Burns, H. L. Burns,
J.J.Burns, William Lohman,
William B. Lohman, R.E.Nelson,
Merion Bradford, Marion Bradford, H. J. Milgreth, H. C. Milgreth,
Howard Milgreth, E. L. Burnes, Ray Hall, Dan Murphy, Chi Karpis,
Raymond Hadley, Labin Karpis, James, Charles M. Bronson, Leroy
Morrison, E.M.Ragner, H.C.Weggoner, Elmer Wagner, E.N.Wagner,
Edward H.Wagner, L.C.Woods, A.S.Green, Ray Green, E.N.Green,
Charles A.Richards, W.B.Lohman, Slim, Raymond Alvin Karpis,
Ray Carson, T.N.Nelson, R.J.Burns, Ray Hadley, R.S.Carson,
F.M.Dawson, R. G. Hayes, Jr.

TITLE OF CASE:
CHARLES JOSEPH FITZGERALD, with aliases;
ALBIN FRANCIS KARPIS, with aliases;
JOHN P. PEIFER, with alias;
EDMUND CONRAD BARTHOLMEY; ARTHUR R. BARKER,
with aliases; WILLIAM BRYAN BOLTON, with
aliases; FRED BARKER (Deceased) with aliases;
FRED C. GOETZ (Deceased), with aliases;
ELMER FARMER. WILLIAM A. HAMM, JR. - Victim.
KIDNAPING.

ALBIN FRANCIS KARPIS, together with other principals in this case,
kidnaped WILLIAM A. HAMM, JR., President of the Theodore Hamm Brewing Company of
St. Paul, Minnesota, at St.Paul on June 15, 1933, and on the same date transported
him via automobile to Bensenville, Illinois, where he was held for ransom in the
amount of $100,000.00. The victim was released near Wyoming, Minnesota, on the
early morning of June 19, 1933 after ransom of $100,000.00 had been collected from
the victim's family.

KARPIS was one of the actual kidnapers and was the driver of the
automobile in which the victim was transported to the hideout. During the period
the victim was held prisoner, KARPIS acted as guard. KARPIS also drove the automobile in which the victim was transported from the hideout in Bensenville,
Illinois, to the point near Wyoming, Minnesota, and released. KARPIS received
between $7,000.00 and $8,000.00 for his participation in this kidnaping.

APPROVED AND FORWARDED:

COPIES OF THIS REPORT FURNISHED TO:
3 - Bureau
2 - Chicago
1 - Cincinnati
2 - St.Paul

SKM:ACF

SPECIAL AGENT IN CHARGE

DO NOT WRITE IN THESE SPACES

RECORDED AND INDEXED:

BUREAU OF INVESTIGATION

CHECKED OFF:

DEPARTMENT OF JUSTICE

JACKETED:

ROUTED TO: FILE:

U. S. GOVERNMENT PRINTING OFFICE: 1935   7—1932

Robert Stroud, the "Birdman of Alcatraz," was the most famous prisoner in America in the 1950s and '60s because of a book and a movie by that name. He studied canaries for 22 years while in prison and wrote numerous articles and two books on bird diseases.

So influential was the 1962 Burt Lancaster portrayal of a wise, patient prisoner scientist, that people signed petitions by the thousands urging the government to parole him. When asked a year before the movie came out why he wanted to get out of prison, the real Robert Stroud, aged 71 at the time, said that he wanted "to kill a number of individuals on his list and had so short a time in which to do it." People who bought the Hollywood myth were astounded, but it was typical Stroud. A tall man with a massive ego and a combustible temper, he believed the shocking truth was a weapon. The public didn't want Robert Stroud paroled, they wanted Burt Lancaster paroled.

There were other problems with the movie. Stroud was not the Birdman of Alcatraz; he was the Birdman of Leavenworth, where he raised canaries from 1920 until 1942. And he wasn't a trained pathologist; he couldn't tell the difference between a bacterial and a viral disease thus he didn't discover nor cure any bird diseases. But he is credited with two of the earliest books on bird diseases printed in the United States, and is more appropriately called an ornithologist, or someone who studies bird behavior.

He was also clinically diagnosed as a psychopath. He lacked a conscience and felt no remorse. In 1909, when he killed a man, the coroner determined that Stroud had executed him as he lay on the floor. (The bullet had entered his temple but exited his abdomen.) Stroud got 12 years, was sent to McNeil Island, then stabbed a prisoner in the back and was sent to Leavenworth. In 1916, a year before he was scheduled to parole out, he fatally stabbed a guard at lunch in front of 1,100 prisoners. Officer Andrew F. Turner had written him up the night before, thus preventing Stroud from a visit with his brother.

Stroud received the death penalty but it was overturned by President Woodrow Wilson. In 1920 the U.S. Attorney General gave him a sentence of "life in solitary confinement." Leavenworth newspapers wondered how such a bright 30-year-old man could be kept idle for life.

The answer came when he found a nest of baby sparrows, nursed them into adulthood, then asked if he could purchase a canary (not unusual in those days). He turned this hobby into a two-decade business in which he

A snowy egret escapes Alcatraz.

bought and sold birds through magazine ads, developed canary feed and wrote articles on bird care.

Stroud gained enormous power in Leavenworth. When Art Dollison first worked there in 1938, the prison was so overcrowded (the 1,100-man facility had ballooned to 3,600 men during the Depression) that some men were sleeping in the aisles. Yet Stroud had two cells, one for his bed, the other for his birds. And the administration had cut a hole in the wall so he could walk room to room. But all this ended in 1942 when he was transferred to Alcatraz and placed in the D block segregation wing.

He was a bright man who was bored while in seg. Others confined there were often emotionally unstable and easy to arouse. On one occasion he caused a riot in D block. In another incident in 1948 prison authorities blamed him for a food strike. They quickly moved him into the prison's hospital, where he remained for 11 years. This was his deepest segregation; for many years he was the only prisoner living there.

In the 1950s, Thomas Gaddis wrote a book about Stroud, which was made into the movie. It was a romantic tale of a patient, caring prisoner identifying and curing bird diseases despite government indifference.

Despite the film's influence, Stroud never got out of prison. Psychologists generally agree that psychopaths cannot be turned around.

He died in the Springfield, Missouri federal medical prison of heart failure on November 21, 1963, one day before President John F. Kennedy was assassinated. He had served 54 years behind bars. Although he got a *New York Times* obituary, his death was quickly overshadowed and his scientific contributions were eventually downgraded.

NARA

Clarence Carnes was 18 years old, 5'9" and 144 pounds when he arrived in 1945. He was scared to death.

He was one of the youngest men sent to Alcatraz and he expected to never get out of prison. While being held in Oklahoma, serving life for a robbery that ended in murder, he escaped three times, twice abducted individuals to escape in their cars and assaulted a jailer. That added a 99-year kidnapping charge and a 5-year escape charge to the life sentence. He went to Leavenworth, then, because of the escapes, to Alcatraz.

In 1946, a few months after he arrived on the Rock, he was involved in the bloodiest escape attempt in its history. Six cons assaulted officers and held them hostage, obtained guns and tried to shoot their way out of the building. Two guards and three prisoners were killed. Two other cons were later executed. Only Carnes' life was spared because of his youth.

But rumors spread that he had turned state's evidence in exchange for his life, and cons who arrived later wanted nothing to do with him. And because guards had also died in the attempt, some officers treated him disdainfully. He was bitter, sullen, withdrawn, and at times verbally or physically assaultive. His file stated that he had few friends, was "extremely tense, morbid and preoccupied." It would take almost a decade before he relaxed.

Carnes spent 17 years on Alcatraz, many of them in D block. He and Stroud became friends there and often played chess together in their separate cells by calling out the numbered spaces. He knew that Stroud, despite his intelligence, had little insight into his own personality, a characteristic of a psychopath.

Eventually, Carnes was released from D block and obtained a job as the library orderly. He was marginally involved in the 1962 Morris-Anglin escape, but was not really interested in trying to go with them.

Carnes was transferred to Leavenworth when Alcatraz closed and got out of prison in 1979.

He worked for Habitat for Humanity in Kansas City where he displayed little of the aggressive behavior that had marked his prison life. In 1980, a movie based on his life, *Alcatraz, The Whole Shocking Story*, was filmed and he had the ironic pleasure of returning to Alcatraz where actors in officer uniforms respectfully called him "Mr. Carnes." At one point he got bored with the slow pace of filming, he said, and fell asleep in a nearby cell, feeling secure and at home.

But Carnes was a sick man throughout the 1980s. He had diabetes, which was complicated by renal disease. And he had also tested positive for AIDs. He was found several times on Kansas City streets, drunk and incoherent. On one occasion he was hospitalized after being mugged. He was a lonely man and his parole officer thought that he genuinely feared life on the outside. In 1986, he stole $800 and left Missouri, telling friends he wanted to feel free at least once in his life. But he'd also become angry when his parole officer thought he still needed supervision. A friend paid most of the money back. But breaking parole made him a fugitive and his ultimate goal may have been to get back into prison for health care. He traveled, was homeless in Los Angeles for a time and eventually returned to prison where he received dialysis for renal problems.

Carnes may have felt comfortable back inside, but he had become a bitter man, at times acting aggressively and indifferent to the staff.

He died in 1988 in the federal prison hospital in Springfield, Missouri two days before he was scheduled to walk out of prison. He was given a pauper's burial. But once again, he was the recipient of a generous gift. According to *The Boston Herald*, former Alcatraz prisoner James "Whitey" Bulger had the body disinterred and transferred to Daisy, Oklahoma where a proper Choctaw service and burial could be held. Bulger reportedly paid $4,000 for the casket, attended the services in 1998 and passed around $100 bills.

Jolene Babyak

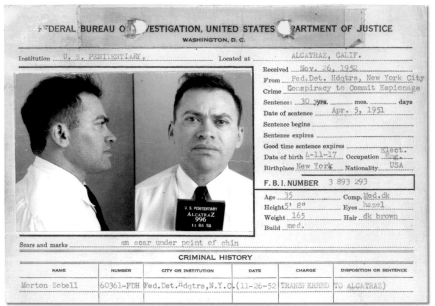

FEDERAL BUREAU OF INVESTIGATION, UNITED STATES DEPARTMENT OF JUSTICE
WASHINGTON, D. C.

Institution __U. S. PENITENTIARY__   Located at __ALCATRAZ, CALIF.__

Received __Nov. 26, 1952__
From __Fed.Det. Hdqtrs, New York City__
Crime __Conspiracy to Commit Espionage__
Sentence: __30 yrs.__ mos. days
Date of sentence __Apr. 5, 1951__
Sentence begins
Sentence expires
Good time sentence expires
Date of birth __4-11-17__ Occupation __Elect. Eng.__
Birthplace __New York__ Nationality __USA__

F. B. I. NUMBER   3 893 293

Age __35__   Comp. __Med.dk__
Height __5' 8"__   Eyes __hazel__
Weight __165__   Hair __dk brown__
Build __med.__

Scars and marks __sm scar under point of chin__

CRIMINAL HISTORY

NAME	NUMBER	CITY OR INSTITUTION	DATE	CHARGE	DISPOSITION OR SENTENCE
Morton Sobell	60361-FDH	Fed.Det.Hdqtrs,N.Y.C.	(11-26-52)	TRANSFERRED TO ALCATRAZ)	

NARA

Morton Sobell was one of the most unique prisoners to ever spend time on Alcatraz. Neither a gangster nor a common criminal, he was convicted of conspiracy to commit espionage in 1951 along with Julius and Ethel Rosenberg in a famous, controversial case.

At the trial, only one man testified against him, telling the court that he had accompanied Sobell to Julius' house to deliver a 35mm film can. The contents of the film can were not revealed. But Sobell had been a member of the Communist Party and had later signed a loyalty oath denying any connection to "subversive" organizations. By 1950, when Joseph McCarthy's House UnAmerican Activities Committee was creating headlines rooting out subversives, Sobell realized he was guilty of perjury and could be compelled to name friends and relatives who had also been party members. He did not testify in his own behalf. And on what analysts today call flimsy evidence, he was sentenced to 30 years.

Although Bureau of Prisons director, James V. Bennett, had earlier told Sobell, "You're not the type of man we send to Alcatraz," he arrived on Wednesday, November 26, 1952, the day before Thanksgiving.

But Sobell was lucky. The Rosenbergs were given the death penalty and electrocuted in Sing Sing on June 19, 1953.

Sobell was unique on Alcatraz because he had a college degree in electrical engineering and had never before served time. That gave him a different perspective.

He spent much of his time in cell C-342, where he had a tiny view of the Golden Gate Bridge. On evenings when it wasn't foggy he could see the sun descend behind the bridge and realized that he would never again have such a magnificent view. He also found both officers and prisoners respectful, some calling him Mr. Sobell. He said that there was no overt brutality on Alcatraz because the prison's population was small and word would get around too fast. But he also found the prison unusually oppressive for the same reason: it was smaller than other institutions, "making for a much greater sameness—in all ways."

The lack of information was one of the greatest tortures—he kept asking why he was on Alcatraz, but he never received an answer. He blamed the prison authorities for withholding facts, but they may not have known. According to FBI documents released later under a Freedom of Information Act request, Roy Cohn, a member of the prosecution team, is the man who suggested Sobell be sent to the Rock. (Cohn was a notorious political operative who made his name as chief council on Senator McCarthy's committee and was disbarred in 1986 for unethical conduct at the same time he was dying of AIDs.)Sobell felt himself growing increasingly self-absorbed and callous on Alcatraz, which he thought was a reaction to his limited life.

He left the Rock in 1958 and transferred to Atlanta. He was finally released from prison in 1969, after serving more than 18 years. Alcatraz was so rigid, he said, that his transfer to Atlanta was a more radical change than walking out of any prison into the free world. Sobell's 1974 book was reprinted in 2001 along with the FBI documents. However, in September 2008, at age 91, he admitted for the first time to the *New York Times* that he had been a soviet spy. He also implicated Julius Rosenberg.

Photograph by George DeVincenzi

In his file someone hinted that Ellsworth Johnson was a legend in his own mind. And certainly he acted the part; he was charismatic, self-assured, he had a deep, rich voice and a commanding presence. And so fearful was his reputation that shooters often missed. "Some years ago," a prison report stated, "enemies shot up a bar and missed him, but killed two bystanders."

In one incident, he was having dinner with writer Helen Lawrenson. Lawrenson was a white woman who protested too much that she wasn't one of those society ladies who trotted up to Harlem in the 1930s for assignations with black jazz musicians and local gangsters; in fact, she wrote for a high style magazine, *Vanity Fair*, by day and hung out with Bumpy by night. Bumpy was about to have a duel with another rival.

"How can you eat?" she asked him.

"I'm hungry," he replied. After one of his men told him all was ready, Bumpy went outside. She waited, her eyes wide, her breath stilled. She heard gunfire. Finally, he walked back in, slid into his chair and ordered up a banana split.

"What happened?" she asked. "Nothin'," he said. "We both missed."

Johnson did get shot in the back in 1934, and he had multiple stab wounds in his chest and abdomen— so he knew the bumps in life—but he always seemed to recover, which lent credence to his legendary reputation.

Born in either 1906 or 1908 (or 1900), he was the seventh child of a seaman and his wife. The family migrated to New York about 1913 where he attended school at least until the age of 14. But Bumpy had a violent temper and began getting arrested in 1924 for felonious assaults.

Over the next 22 years, he was arrested at least 15 times for assaults, robberies, grand larceny and stabbings, serving more than 16 years in New York prisons at Elmira, Rikers Island and Sing Sing. He became involved in the Harlem numbers rackets. A simple scheme: betters would put a penny, a dime or a dollar on a number from 1 to 999 and whatever number came up, paid off. When a popular number hit and the "policy banks" couldn't pay off, big-time mobster "Dutch" Schultz swooped in and took over. But Schultz, whose real name was Arthur Flegenheimer, was murdered in 1935 by his own mob. A 1997 film, *Hoodlum*, starring Lawrence Fishburne was loosely based on Bumpy's Harlem story.

When Johnson got out of Sing Sing in 1947 he took over a policy bank, then moved into the more lucrative drug trade.

If you want to guess who aided jazz legend Charlie Parker's final descent into heroin addiction, you could do no worse than point to Bumpy; he may have been one of the hipper suppliers in Harlem at that time. But maybe not that careful. In 1951, he sold two ounces of heroin to a Bureau of Narcotics undercover agent for $450. Two days later, he was nabbed in another heroin sale. These crimes plus his history got him a 15-year sentence in 1953. He was sent to Leavenworth, then in 1954 to Alcatraz.

"An immaculate dresser, egotistical to the extreme," stated one report, "and when encouraged to talk about himself, actually reveals information which rebounds to his detriment."

When Johnson arrived on the Rock, he may have looked as he once described himself, "like a little fly in a bowl of milk," because only about 6 to 10 percent of the prison's population was black. Over the years, however, the black population grew to 25 percent with Johnson as the acknowledged leader.

NARA

He seemed to have the respect of everyone. He was intelligent, had nearly a high school-equivalent education (most were 6th to 8th grade) and was well-read. According to his file, on Alcatraz he subscribed to *Newsweek*, *Look*, *Life*, *The New Yorker*, *Time*, *Jet* and *Ebony* magazines. He was described as pleasant, respectful, active and energetic. Although he left Alcatraz in 1958 for Atlanta, he was returned less than a year later for being a "disturbing influence." Once back on the Rock, however, he became one of the better behaved prisoners whose attitude and actions were said to have a calming influence on the younger prisoners.

Johnson was paroled in the mid-1960s. The man who thought he was invincible was felled by a heart attack in his early 60s while eating dinner with friends in New York City. He was out on bail for yet another indictment for importing drugs from Peru.

A legend in his own mind? According to the *New York Times*, 1,200 people attended his funeral in July 1968.

U. S. PENITENTIARY
ALCATRAZ
1518
7 28 61

Santa Fe's "Super Chief" Traveling thru the Orange Groves, California

Cohen 1518

The Mini Mobster

Mickey Cohen 1913 – 1976

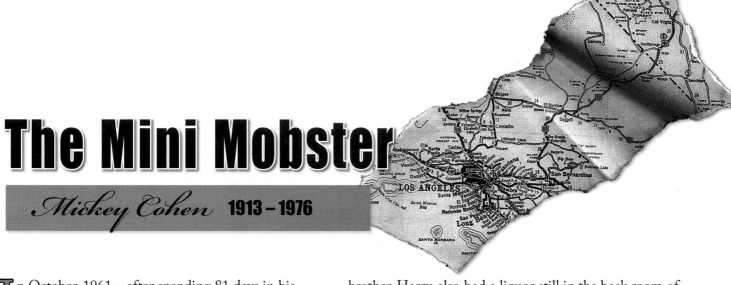

In October, 1961—after spending 81 days in his little five-by-nine foot cell on a 15-year sentence for income tax evasion—Mickey Cohen walked off the Rock and went to the Fairmont Hotel.

It was the shortest, most spectacular transfer any Alcatraz prisoner ever made. The Fairmont, at the crest of Nob Hill, is one of the swankiest hotels in San Francisco. As news reporters surrounded him, Mickey got a shave and a haircut in the hotel's barbershop. He told them he didn't know why he'd been sent to Alcatraz and bragged that he wasn't going back. Oops, he lost his appeal, and was back on the Rock seven months later.

It was all downhill from there.

But it had been a steep slide most of his life. Meyer Harris Michael "Mickey" Cohen was the youngest of six children born in 1913 in New York City to Russian immigrants, Max and Frannie Cohen. His father died shortly before he was two, which threw his family into poverty. Then his mother, Frannie, developed a "tension in the throat and a hoarseness" that lasted for years and may have been "hysterical in nature," meaning it was psychological. Because of her health, the family moved to Los Angeles and settled into a poor neighborhood. To help out, Mickey began selling newspapers on the street by age five or six.

He was a cute little kid and not afraid of anybody. Early hustling lessons began when a delivery boy bargained with him for hot dogs and bologna. "See, I used to bring home a lot of my own food," he wrote in his book, *Mickey Cohen, In My Own Words*. Prohibition hit and guys would give him a quarter to hide a bottle of liquor. His older

brother, Harry, also had a liquor still in the back room of a drugstore they operated. Mickey claimed he got nailed for bootlegging when he was only nine years old.

Facts about his education are sketchy. He was sent to a "special" school, which may have been for delinquents or mentally retarded kids. But he hated it, learned little and quit by the time he was ten.

Instead, he concentrated on working the better street corners, then he began hanging out in pool halls where he racked up sets for quarters. That led to boxing, where he sometimes earned $20 a bout. Mickey spent money on cool clothes even then.

Older brother, Harry, was a "rough hustler," whose gimmick was to go to sports arenas, act like a boss, and walk away with money from unsuspecting cashiers. Harry moved to Cleveland, Ohio, Mickey followed, and Harry began promoting his kid brother as a boxer. Mickey later said that the boxing ring and the rackets were one and the same. Indeed, one big fight promoter was Frankie Carbo, a man Mickey would later know on Alcatraz.

The Depression hit when Mickey was 16. He had no education, no skills and he found boxing a tough way to make a living. That's when the "little pugilist" became the "little mobster."

For the next 10 years he floated from Cleveland to New York to Chicago becoming increasingly involved with underworld gambling. Mickey was good with his fists and even better with a gun. He claimed to have met Al Capone; whether it was true or not, it was his way of saying that the baton had been passed to him. (Although

People were killed

and Mickey was usually in the washroom rinsing his hands.

Los Angeles Public Library

he was the only one who thought so.) He took on the air of the bigger Mafia dons' lavish generosity, which anesthetized his family from asking too many questions.

By 1939, when he was 26, he returned to Los Angeles. He claimed he was sent by the East Coast Mafia to monitor "Bugsy" Siegel, who was then building the Las Vegas Flamingo Hotel. For the next 13 years he solidified power around his gambling operations and got his name constantly in the newspaper.

Mickey was a good looking man in the 1940s, impeccably groomed in expensive clothing. But the closer you got the more neurotic he seemed. Uneducated, with a limited vocabulary, he had little insight and was full of anxieties. As long as he was in control, his neurosis was in check. But once he lost control, he would whine, cajole and pout. And unfortunately, he was a man with a gun.

> **Mickey was neurotic, self-absorbed and armed with a gun.**

At 5'6", at times ballooning to 165 pounds, he was childlike in his need for approval. He'd talk to anyone and say anything, which made him popular with Los Angeles reporters. They called him "the dapper little hoodlum," or "the paunchy little gangster," treating him like he was a pampered sports figure. He favored "zoot suits" with cuffed trousers and jackets with wide lapels and massive shoulder pads. He invited photographers to his home to show off his room-size closets with rows of expensively tailored suits, which he gave away after the first dry cleaning. He owned more than 600 pairs of French lisle socks. He had scores of hats all lined up in boxes. He wore spectator shoes, snake skin boots and, when the occasion called, riding breeches. Even when lounging at home with his wife, LaVonne, he was well turned out.

He was also the focus of numerous Los Angeles police investigations. Beginning in 1939, and for many years, he was regularly arrested for robbery, assault with a deadly weapon and bookmaking. He thought nothing of beating up rivals. In May '45, he was arrested for the murder of Maxie Shaman, a competitive bookie. "Well, there was a shooting," he wrote, "And he got it." Self-defense, he claimed, and the cops couldn't prove otherwise. He later bragged that it cost $40,000 to dodge that one.

In May '46 he was questioned and released in the murder of bookie Paul Gibbons. Police understood that Cohen had put a contract out on Gibbons, then "liquidated" the two subcontractors.

Benjamin "Bugsy" Siegel was murdered in '47. He'd

Mickey's house was bombed *and he was photo-graphed lamenting the prized suits he would now give away.*

been shot through the window of a mansion while reading a newspaper. "Naturally I missed Benny," Mickey wrote, "But to be honest with you, his getting knocked in was not a bad break for me." Mickey took over part of his operation. Then colleague Harry "Hookie" Rothman was fatally shot in the face. Mickey was in the building but he was in the bathroom rinsing his hands.

In July '49, Mickey and his entourage were attacked outside Sherry's Cafe in Hollywood. Neddie Herbert, who had taken over "Hookie" Rothman's business, was killed, and Mickey and two others were wounded. "How any human being could fire bullets into a crowd beats me," Mickey exclaimed to reporters. "They're animals. They ain't human." Then two of Cohen's bodyguards disappeared, and Mickey later wrote that their bodies were taken to the lime pit where they dissolved. Interestingly, they were going to testify against him in an upcoming trial.

That same year his serialized life story ran in the *Los Angeles Daily News.*

Then Cohen's attorney, with whom he had a falling out, was murdered in front of his own home. Quickly, Mickey's home was bombed. His neighbors demanded that he move but he waved

them off; he was a simple businessman, he claimed, running a haberdashery called "Michael's." But police noted that it featured a bullet-proof steel door and did a nominal amount of business.

Finally in July 1951, he was sentenced by the feds to five years for income tax evasion and sent to McNeil Island. His downfall, he later reasoned, was paying his taxes the *first* time. "Once you start paying them, you got to keep paying them."

McNeil was the other federal prison island (now it's a state prison). Sometimes guys who screwed up there were sent to Alcatraz. Mickey stayed out of trouble.

He was popular with inmates but an administrative nightmare. Excitable, at times depressed and resentful, he was a poor worker who constantly had to be supervised. He badgered staff for job changes and special favors and became hostile when corrected. He had "an almost compulsive urge to attract attention to himself," an early report stated. And he had a little tic—he washed his hands constantly. Mickey was released in October 1955 and McNeil was happy to get rid of him.

He returned to his former life at a frantic pace. He moved in with his wife, LaVonne, in her $85 a month apartment, he filed articles of incorporation for "Michael's Greenhouse," declared himself a salesman and resumed his lavish dinner parties at posh L.A. restaurants. Then he split with LaVonne and moved into the Del Capri Hotel apartments on Wilshire Boulevard, where the rent was $7,700 a year—more than most people *earned* in a year. He divorced LaVonne and, according to later prison reports, gave her $1 a month in alimony.

Despite his obvious cash flow, he filed tax returns in 1956 and '57 showing earnings of less than $2,500, half of which he claimed was his wife's. To inquisitive probation officers he claimed his money came from "gifts" and

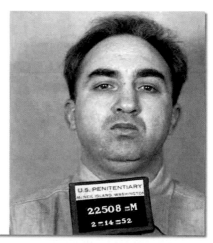

Mickey at McNeil Island in 1952. They were glad to get rid of him.

AP/Wide World Photos

Like a wounded bird, *Mickey turns toward Sandy Hagen as he was about to be imprisoned for income tax evasion. Sandy had inadvertently helped convict him and visited him on Alcatraz numerous times.*

other famous people like Jerry Lewis, Red Skelton and Jimmy Durante's manager. He flirted with Christianity, and later famed evangelist Bill Graham wrote letters in his behalf to prison authorities. Washington columnist, Drew Pearson, even wrote numerous letters, which are in Mickey's prison file.

He began taking up with younger and younger women. "Beverly Hills" was the name of one friend. He was seen with "Candy Barr," a stripper he helped when she had trouble with a Texas marijuana charge. He dated a teenage waitress, Claretta Hashagan, who called herself Sandy Hagen. She was with him at a dinner party at Rondelli's Restaurant in December 1959, when, a few feet away, Jack "The Enforcer" Whalen was fatally shot. Cohen was booked on suspicion of that murder too, but released because none of the 30 or so diners could remember anything specific. "To paraphrase Winston Churchill," the L.A. police chief fumed, "never before did so few see so little."

In May 1961, the feds again took him to trial for income tax evasion. According to Jernnings' *Saturday Evening Post* article, he "wisecracked, sulked, raged and came close to tears" during the proceedings. Key among the evidence that sent him to prison was jewelry that Sandy told cops she had. Sandy, of course, visited Mickey numerous times while he was on Alcatraz, much to the

"loans."

In 1957, his sister allegedly purchased the Carousel Ice Cream Parlor and Mickey became the public relations man. But like the Greenhouse, it became the office through which cycled numerous underworld characters. He traveled to New York, San Francisco, Washington, D.C. and Philadelphia—always staying at top hotels. Yet, in 1958, he reported no income at all.

In a later *Saturday Evening Post* article, writer Dean Jennings said he "saw wardrobe closets filled with 1,500 pairs of socks, 50 pairs of $50 silk pajamas, and neckties by the hundreds. It was clear Cohen was spending more than $100,000 a year." Even the government estimated his post-penitentiary scale of living "has been $100,000 to $150,000 annually."

Mickey, in fact, was scamming well-known people. He sold "interest" in a book and movie about his life that he claimed well-known author and movie producer Ben Hecht was writing. He parlayed that into "loans" from

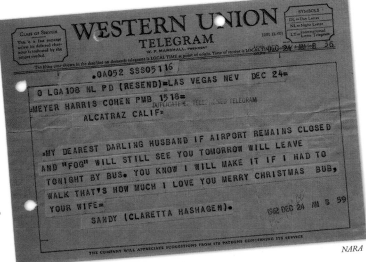

NARA

It was not clear they were married, but very clear that she was afraid of him.

criticism put Blackwell at times on the defensive. "I can assure you that a far greater variety and quantity of food is available for your brother," he wrote once, "than I have available in my own home." Indeed, Alcatraz was known among prisoners for its good food, but for Mickey, the Alcatraz cuisine was probably a step down. Blackwell would not be the only warden to become defensive. Harry's cascade of letters—typed, single-spaced in ALL CAPS on legal-sized paper, *SOMETIMES IN RED*—with bitter, racist opinions and scattershot accusations, showed that he clearly couldn't control himself. When Mickey was in Springfield later, the warden wrote an apology to Harry for not being home when Harry called. It was extraordinary that the man would call the warden at his home.

"Relationships between Mr. Cohen and his family seem to be characterized by effusive sentimentality and mutual exploitation," one report stated. "Correspondence has been voluminous and requires careful review."

Mickey left Alcatraz the second time on February 26, 1963, and was transferred to Atlanta penitentiary. Six months later he was attacked by a prisoner. Berl Estes McDonald was a clinically diagnosed sociopath, serving 10 years for postal robbery, who had attacked a prisoner in Leavenworth, which got him transferred to Alcatraz as AZ 1542. After both he and

Mickey says goodbye *one more time as he peeks out of the boat on his way back to Alcatraz.*

AP/Wide World Photos

breathless anticipation of everyone on the island. She was 19, and no doubt hoping that her devotion to him would be her life insurance.

After Mickey's initial 81 days on the Rock, and his quick tour of San Francisco, his appeal failed and he returned to Alcatraz in May 1962. For the first time in his life he growled at reporters.

While prison is a good setting for some—Karpis for example, eventually turned his life around—it would be devastating to Mickey Cohen. His neurosis accelerated and his lower lip, which had always protruded, now became more pronounced.

Alcatraz Warden Olin G. Blackwell did not look forward to Mickey's return. Mickey got scads of letters, telegrams and postcards. Chief among his correspondents was his also increasingly erratic brother, Harry. Mickey would whine about the food, Harry would write a complaining letter to the warden and Blackwell would write back in a businesslike tone. But the constant

Photograph by William (Bill) Long, Jr.

Warden Olin G. Blackwell, above left, was the last warden of Alcatraz and had the pleasure of Mickey Cohen's residency. Here he stands with Captain Tom Bradley, an unknown officer, and, at the far right, Lt. Lloyd Miller.

Cohen transferred to Atlanta, McDonald scaled a wall, picked up a lead pipe about two feet in length and bashed Cohen's head from behind. Apparently, Mickey had refused McDonald's request for money to buy a guitar. Mickey crumbled to the ground and would never be the same.

The top of his skull was fractured, requiring a six-hour surgery during which it was fitted with a metal plate.

Months of rehabilitation improved his bladder and bowel functions, but he would never again walk without the aid of a walker or a cane, and became, in the words of his brother Harry, "hopelessly crippled."

He was transferred to the Springfield Medical Center on October 10, 1963. He sued the government and won a modest settlement.

For the first time in his prison career, he was given a battery of educational, intellectual and psychological tests. He couldn't recite the alphabet, didn't know the sequence of months and couldn't divide or multiply. He claimed he had never learned. Authorities didn't know which came first, his brain injury or his educational deficits. But Mickey was profoundly ignorant, and had always sought out sympathetic friends who could cover for him.

Mickey Cohen had a number of problems but the most obvious was his obsessive-compulsive personality disorder (OCD). Toward the end of his life he steadily deteriorated. By his own admission he washed his hands every two to three minutes. He claimed he used six rolls of toilet paper a day to clean up around himself. Springfield authorities wanted to transfer him to another prison but knew that he would need to cell near a shower because he showered daily for about an hour and a half. That was a big part of the problem, in fact. Mickey would

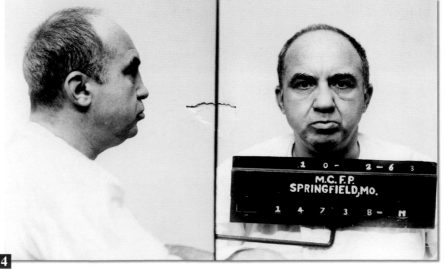

Mickey Cohen arrives in Atlanta penitentiary but the worst is yet to come (1). Berl McDonald (2), who had also transferred from Alcatraz, attacked Mickey with a pipe. McDonald fractured Mickey's skull and surgeons cleaned up the damage and put in a metal plate in a six-hour operation (3). Mickey was moved from Atlanta penitentiary to Springfield, Missouri (4), in October 1963—the federal prisons' medical facility. Many Alcatraz prisoners ended up in Springfield, because they needed an operation, medical attention or therapy. Mickey appeared tired and unfocused.

complain to Harry that he wasn't getting enough good food. Harry would write belligerent letters to the warden, who would patiently explain that Mickey often missed meals because he was showering so much. This is a key to Mickey's personality—these arguments never had a solution and were a part of his little madness.

"Cohen continues to be an egocentric individual with a severe cleanliness neurosis," his release report stated in 1971, "He requires a great deal of patience and understanding and at times can become very provoking. If on release he is unable to maintain his self image of an important influential man, it may result in severe emotional deterioration."

OCD is an anxiety disorder. In Mickey's case it could be traced to his newspaper days when he frequently washed the printer's ink from his hands. But his mother, who was immaculately clean, may have had a similar disorder. Psychologically, of course, Mickey also had blood on his hands. Which may mean that he wasn't a psychopath—a small enough concession for all the trouble he caused.

But Mickey's story is as sad as the others. With no education and an older, unstable brother who was a small-time crook, Mickey came of age at the beginning of the worst economic decade in modern history. Increasingly he was ill-equipped to pick up a legitimate skill. And he got a taste of the high life, which is intoxicating and makes anyone feel as if the good times will last forever. They don't. In the end, if he had any insight at all, he must have felt like life had been rigged against him.

He got out of prison in January 1972, but the world had changed. He had gone in before President John F. Kennedy was assassinated and come out when the nation was undergoing the Vietnam War and the social-equality protests. As predicted, he no longer felt important.

In one more bid for publicity, he inserted himself into the 1974 Patty Hearst kidnapping, claiming that his contacts in Cleveland told him where she could be found. He urged her father to go in with guns, but Hearst declined. Mickey's long-awaited book came out in 1975, but it was badly written and sold poorly.

He died July 29, 1976 of stomach cancer. He was 63.

Courtesy of Phil Dollison

An unknown correspondent sent a postcard to Mickey Cohen at Alcatraz. It depicted a cafeteria tray with the four food groups and a note on the back, that said, "Dear Mick, Empire crumbling. Help."

At their mother's funeral, Mickey is being helped by his older brother, Harry, second from the left, who may have been his downfall.

AP/Wide World Photos

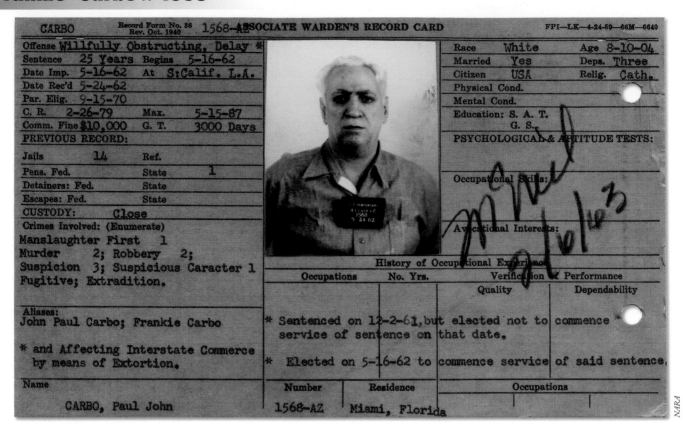

CARBO	Record Form No. 36 Rev. Oct. 1940	1568-AZ	ASSOCIATE WARDEN'S RECORD CARD		FPI—LK—4-24-59—66M—6640

Offense Willfully Obstructing, Delay *
Sentence 25 Years   Begins 5-16-62
Date Imp. 5-16-62   At St.Calif. L.A.
Date Rec'd 5-24-62
Par. Elig. 9-15-70
C. R. 2-26-79   Max. 5-15-87
Comm. Fine $10,000   G. T. 3000 Days
PREVIOUS RECORD:

Jails 14   Ref.
Pens. Fed.   State 1
Detainers: Fed.   State
Escapes: Fed.   State
CUSTODY: Close
Crimes Involved: (Enumerate)
Manslaughter First   1
Murder   2; Robbery   2;
Suspicion 3; Suspicious Caracter 1
Fugitive; Extradition.

Aliases:
John Paul Carbo; Frankie Carbo

* and Affecting Interstate Commerce
  by means of Extortion.

Race White   Age 8-10-04
Married Yes   Deps. Three
Citizen USA   Relig. Cath.
Physical Cond.
Mental Cond.
Education: S. A. T.
    G. S.
PSYCHOLOGICAL & APTITUDE TESTS:

Occupational Skills:

Avocational Interests:

History of Occupational Experience
Occupations   No. Yrs.   Verification   Performance   Quality   Dependability

* Sentenced on 12-2-61, but elected not to commence
  service of sentence on that date.

* Elected on 5-16-62 to commence service of said sentence.

Name	Number	Residence	Occupations
CARBO, Paul John	1568-AZ	Miami, Florida	

Paul John "Frankie" Carbo was a piece of work. Known as an expert hired assassin for "Murder Incorporated," the enforcement arm of the Syndicate run by Louie "Lepke" Buchalter and Albert Anastasia, Carbo was a disarmingly soft-spoken man who rose to become the "czar of boxing" in the 1940s and '50s. He controlled much of the boxing world through terror.

He was one of the last of the top-flight racketeers to be convicted, getting 25 years for extortion in 1961. Born in 1904 in New York City, he was the first of five children of Italian immigrants. His criminal career began in 1922 when he was 18, and eventually included five murder indictments. Over the years it was said that he was involved in the murders of "Bugsy" Siegel and Harry "Big Greenie" Greenberg. But witnesses against him had a habit of disappearing or dying (as did Abe "Kid Twist" Reles, who fell to his death from a hotel window while being guarded by police.) He served two short prison terms in the New York City jail at Rikers Island and Sing Sing state prison. He married three times, had a daughter with cerebral palsy, but never seemed to be at home.

What prosecutors knew and could prove were sharply divided. He traveled often to Boston, Washington, D.C., Miami, Chicago and Los Angeles. He seemed to travel with no luggage (or at least never carried it) and was adept at checking a room for listening devices. His accomplices read like a who's who of the underworld. According to an investigator, Carbo held court in restaurants, often picked up the tab and "No one turns their back on him."

For 30 years he controlled hoodlums who ran professional boxing. He got 50 percent of any fighter he managed and equally hefty percentages from fights that were staged. No one dared plan a match without first clearing it with Carbo. Among his stable of boxers was heavyweight champion Sonny Liston and welter-weight champion Don Jordan. Fight promoters considered him a necessary evil and felt that he brought a semblance of order to the boxing world. Nonetheless he was recorded telling one manager that if his fee wasn't paid, he "would gouge his eyes out."

Carbo was sent to Alcatraz in May 1962. He was considered a "cool, shrewd, calculating" man who "very carefully ponders the questions asked and then very deliberately offers an evasive reply."

Carbo was a model prisoner, polite and popular, serving in Alcatraz, McNeil Island, Atlanta and finally Marion, Illinois. He remained in prison until 1976, working finally as a window washer. He was paroled at age 72 in June 1976 with extensive health problems including congestive heart failure and diabetes. He died five months later in Miami, Florida.

NARA Wash. D.C./Polly Pettit

Irving Wexler, known as "Waxy Gordon" was the most famous prisoner to die on Alcatraz who was not officially registered there, hence his number: A-1.

Stories also differ as to how Wexler actually got his nickname. It was said he was such a slick pickpocket early in life that his fingers were as smooth as wax. But others say it was just a New York way of saying "Wexy." The latter may be more accurate since Waxy spent as much time in prison as out, proving that he wasn't that slick.

Born in 1888, he started stealing early in life and eventually served time in New York, Boston and Philadelphia jails for pick-pocketing. He also spent two years in Sing Sing for assault and robbery.

Described as self-satisfied, suave and "an outstanding conniver," he got into the beer business at the start of Prohibition and rose to become one of the most powerful New York bootleggers. Arnold Rothstein—who was rumored to have fixed the 1919 World Series—was Wexler's financier.

Wexler took over two rival breweries in northern New Jersey in late 1929 about the same time both owners conveniently turned up dead. At the peak of his career, he was said to have eight breweries and was doing a huge business trucking beer to New Jersey and New York. He reported an income of $8,125 in 1930 and $35,000 in 1931, for which he paid slightly more than $3,000 in taxes. Federal tax investigators were later able to determine that he was actually pulling in more than a half million dollars in those two years.

During the investigation, records disappeared, books were rewritten, two witnesses were threatened and several others disappeared. Frustrated investigators reportedly worked for three years, checking with barrel makers and truck agencies to show his true income. While under indictment, Wexler was in the Elizabeth, New Jersey hotel where "Big Maxey" Greenberg, one of his lieutenants, was shot to death, most likely by the "Dutch"

NPS/GGNRA Museum Collection GOGA 12439

Alcatraz prisoners were not allowed to have playing cards, so they adapted dominoes to play various games.

Schultz gang. Wexler escaped by leaping from the window.

Thomas E. Dewey, later governor of New York and presidential candidate, prosecuted Wexler's case. He was able to convince witnesses to testify against Waxy although they were obviously reluctant to speak in the courtroom. Nonetheless, the evidence was overwhelming and the jury took only 40 minutes to find him guilty.

In 1934 Wexler went to federal prisons on a 10-year sentence for income tax evasion. Out in 1940, he was soon involved in the black market of World War II sugar rationing, for which he got another year in prison.

In the late 1940s and early '50s he was involved in narcotics, notably with the "Purple Gang" in Detroit. In 1951, he was caught trying to sell drugs to an undercover agent. He was convicted in New York in December 1951 for two terms of 25-years to life, and sent to Sing Sing and Attica.

Then, because he was awaiting trial in San Francisco on another narcotics charge, he was moved to Alcatraz. When he arrived on May 26, 1952, he was 64 years old, 5'5", 200 pounds and already suffering from heart trouble. Less than a month later, on June 24, in the prison hospital, he slumped in his chair while playing dominoes and died a few minutes later.

ENTERING

ANNX ❦ 1807

SOUTH BOSTON

BULGER holds FBi HoSTAGE

Crime and Politics

James "Whitey" Bulger 1929 – ????

Meet James "Whitey" Bulger, the modern-day, stripped down Al Capone.

While Capone ran around in three-piece suits and monogrammed shirts, had a wife and kid and kept the violence out of the 'hood, Bulger wore jeans and ball caps, never married and preyed on the neighborhood. In the 1930s the crime of the day was transporting liquor. By Bulger's time in the 1970s, '80 and '90s it was drug trafficking, especially the cocaine and crack trade. (Of course gambling, extortion and murder rounded out both their resumes.)

Like bookends, Capone served the first four and a half years Alcatraz was opened and Bulger served during the final four and a half years. But as an added bonus, Bulger's story continues until today and shows how little things have changed. A fugitive since 1995, he's currently on the FBI's Most Wanted list for $2 million.

Like the Chicago mobster's story, Bulger's is so outrageous, that it took the cooperation of several of Boston's FBI agents to accomplish. They were so helpful, in fact, that one former, decorated agent, John Connolly, was given a 10-year sentence for obstruction of justice and racketeering, and was also indicted for conspiracy for murder. Connolly's boss in the Boston FBI, John Morris, who admitted under oath that he took $7,000 in cash from Bulger and his crime partner, Stevie "The Rifleman" Flemmi, turned state's evidence for leniency. Another agent, H. Paul Rico, was arrested by Oklahoma and Florida authorities in October 2003. And others from the Boston FBI came under scrutiny.

But wait! There's more. Whitey's younger brother, William (Billy) Bulger, was a powerful Massachusetts state senator for 35 years while Whitey was a gangster. He was president of the senate, in fact, for longer than any politician in recent Massachusetts history. His story is a rags-to-riches tale that infuriates and enthralls people because of its potential wickedness.

The tendency is to think that a powerful state politician who had a gangster for a brother, would use the brother to his advantage. But Billy Bulger seemed able to take care of his own grudges. According to *Boston Globe* reporters Dick Lehr and Gerald O'Neill, who later wrote a book about Whitey, when one local judge referred to Senator Bulger as a "corrupt midget," Bulger introduced legislation that cut the judge's pay, reduced his staff and shunted his department into another branch of the judiciary. The move failed, but never let it be said that Billy Bulger didn't have a sense of humor.

The state senator and the gangster implicated in 18 murders were a powerful duo from the 1970s until the end of the century. There are reports—denied by Billy—that at least on several occasions the senator slipped across the street from his home to the house of Stevie Flemmi's mother, where he had a cozy dinner with Stevie, Whitey and the two FBI agents, Connolly and Morris.

Flemmi was a piece of work. A former army paratrooper, and tough guy partner in crime with Whitey for many years, Flemmi turned state's witness and testified in court about some of their doings. Twice he seduced teenage girls then discarded them. Debra Davis simply vanished. The other, Deborah Hussey, whom Flemmi had system with an eight-to-ten lane underground expressway. But of course district attorneys, police investigators, city morgue personnel and other knowing wags could use it as a metaphor for the Bulger affair.

It's safe to say that Senator Bulger probably didn't know any of these bloody details. From his book, he appears to remain happily in denial, blaming the media or those who use their get-out-of-jail card to spread rumors and just wishing the whole thing would not contaminate his own family.

In 1995 he retired from the senate chamber and became the president of the University of Massachusetts. The university did well during his tenure and Bulger did well too. But after he was subpoenaed to testify before a House Committee on Governmental Abuse in late 2002 and refused to answer questions on the whereabouts of his brother, he was relieved of his post with nearly a $1 million severance package and reportedly a $250,000 yearly retirement. The public outcry was palpable.

But a far more powerful duo than Whitey and his politically assured brother, was Whitey and Boston FBI agent John Connolly.

They grew up in the same tightknit, hardscrabble Irish immigrant neighborhood of South Boston, known as "Southie." Connolly was younger, impressionable, and taken with the older James Bulger, who seemed to exhibit the same attractive characteristics as many psychopaths—he was focused and ruthless—attracting followers who admired his insolence and fast cars. Whitey was in trouble from an early age; he was tagged numerous times for speeding, he always seemed to have money and he was arrested for robbery in 1947 when he was 18. According to later prison reports, Bulger's father was a strict disciplinarian who on occasion beat him. His father was arrested for assault with a revolver once but the case was dismissed; he also had an arrest for drunkenness.

Connolly lost sight of Bulger as the rowdy teenager got older and moved further afield from the neighborhood. Bulger joined the military. He was arrested twice in 1950, once for Absence Without Leave. In 1951 he was detained for suspicion of rape. Remarkably, he was honorably discharged in 1954. Two years later, he was sentenced to 20 years for bank robberies in Indiana, Massachusetts

AP/Wide World Photos

Former state senator, *and later University of Massachusetts president, Billy Bulger, takes the Fifth Amendment before a 2002 Congressional hearing. He subsequently lost his job but with a nice pension.*

> One—a powerful state senator, the other—a gangster. The Bulger brothers ran South Boston.

helped raise since she was three while he was living with her mother, became intimate with him as a teenager. She talked too much, however, and threatened to reveal their relationship. She was strangled in 1985 at age 26 and buried. Later, because Bulger and Flemmi feared her body would be found, they dug her up and reburied her along with two others—Arthur Barrett, killed in '83, and John McIntyre, killed in '84. In early 2000, authorities were led to the burial site by Kevin Weeks, another gang member who had also decided to testify. Flemmi is now serving a life sentence.

The "Big Dig" is what Bostonians called their huge urban excavation—said to be the biggest engineering feat in American history—which replaced their elevated highway and Rhode Island. In one incident, he carried a .22 revolver and forced two employees to lie on the floor, while he and his accomplices escaped in a stolen vehicle with $42,112. They were caught and convicted.

Bulger arrived at the U.S. Penitentiary in Atlanta in 1956, where he presented a conflicting record. He was a good, dependable worker. He volunteered for medical tests, including tests on LSD research conducted by Emory University and the U.S. Public Health Service. But he also provided hacksaw blades for a friend's escape attempt. Because of that he was transferred to Alcatraz on November 16, 1959 as AZ #1428. His mug shot shows a sullen and defiant man with dark hair. Within five years his hair would turn white, earning him the nickname "Whitey."

Bulger was extremely bright and cagey. He was respectful of authority and said all the right things. It's interesting to view his file in light of what occurred later.

Comments like "anxious to make a new start," and "expresses great respect and love for his family and says will never again cause them shame and humiliation by any of his deeds . . ." occur throughout his file and show that cons at times told authorities (or themselves) what they

AP/Wide World Photos

Crime boss James "Whitey" Bulger

was part of the Winter Hill gang involved in extortion, narcotics distribution, money laundering, murder and possibly arms smuggling.

NARA

thought everyone wanted to hear. "Uses no profanity and doesn't like to hear it," wrote Superintendent of Industries, Art Dollison, about Bulger in one classification meeting, "Dislikes hearing disparaging remarks about religion, country and women." Bulger left Alcatraz when it closed and was transferred to Leavenworth and then Lewisburg, Pennsylvania.

His real crime career began after he paroled out of prison in 1965. He moved into his old apartment with his mother, to whom he seemed devoted. Within several years he was involved with one of Southie's bookmakers, Donald Killeen, whom he later had killed. Throughout the '70s, he was involved in horse race fixing along the East Coast as a member of the Winter Hill gang, a loosely defined Irish mob. They ran South Boston, while the Italian Mafia ran the north side.

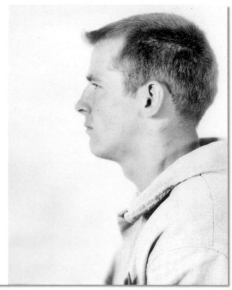

Bulger at USP Atlanta, 1956, looking quite worried. NARA

Bulger's younger neighborhood friend, John Connolly, went in the other direction. After college and law school he joined the FBI in 1968. He worked in Baltimore, San Francisco and New York, but was anxious to return to Boston. Finally, he was asked to help develop Bulger as an informant. The FBI was into its nationwide push to break up the Italian Mafia, and it was felt that

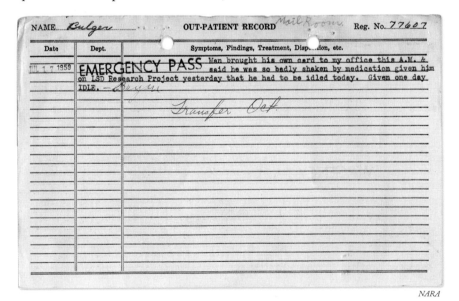

NARA

Bulger participated in LSD experiments conducted at USP Atlanta along with Emory University. It doesn't appear from files that Alcatraz ever had such experiments, partly because the population was too small and the prison had little outside contact.

Whitey and Flemmi, who was handled by H. Paul Rico, could help the effort. Connolly eagerly agreed to return to Boston and took over Bulger as his source.

Handling informants, especially big time gangsters, is a treacherous and often duplicitous arrangement. The test for handlers is to keep their sources from racking up too many serious crimes while providing the FBI with marketable information. But criminals tend to rat out or rub out their enemies to clear a path for themselves. Connolly failed his part of the test. Known around the office as "Cannoli" or "Vino" because of his glib, flashy style, increasingly he became a fan of "Whitey" Bulger as a means for his own career advancement. Or, as reporters Lehr and O'Neill put it, "he went native." He, and later his boss John Morris, began tipping off Bulger and Flemmi to wiretaps, to incoming indictments and to information from other informants—tips which in some cases led to murder. In the meantime, the crooks were able to earn vast sums of money through extortion, gambling, murders, drug deals and maybe even arms smuggling.

John Connolly once telephoned Alcatraz. This was before his serious legal problems and imprisonment. He was just a "retired FBI agent" writing a book and running down a story about another former Alcatraz prisoner, Clarence Carnes. Carnes and Bulger had struck up a friendship on Alcatraz and sources had told the *Boston Herald* later that Bulger had once said that Carnes

Photograph by Officer William (Bill) Long, Jr.

Alcatraz was the top maximum-security federal prison in the country with minimum privileges and a maximum ratio of officers to prisoners. Here an armed officer patrols on the Road Tower, with catwalks to the prison yard wall and the vast San Francisco skyline to his back. At night, or on foggy days, this was a brutal watch with stiff winds coming in from the Pacific Ocean.

may have saved his life. Apparently Carnes, a Choctaw Indian, had also mentioned that he hoped one day he would be buried on Indian land. Instead, when he died in 1988, Carnes was given a pauper's grave in Springfield, Missouri. Bulger found out about it, had his body disinterred and reburied in Daisy, Oklahoma. Sources told the *Herald* that Bulger paid for a $4,000 casket. In relating the story during the telephone call to Alcatraz, Connolly actually called Bulger—then wanted on 18 counts of murder—a "Robin Hood kind of guy." Robbing the rich to give to the poor is a nice myth these guys like to perpetuate. Stolen money is just easier to spend. It was disturbing to hear an FBI agent even state such a thing.

Over the years Whitey amassed millions of dollars in illegal activities. Although he didn't do drugs and seldom even drank, he allegedly extorted money from drug deals in the neigh-

At Alcatraz in 1959, where he said his actions would never again bring shame and humiliation on his family. NARA

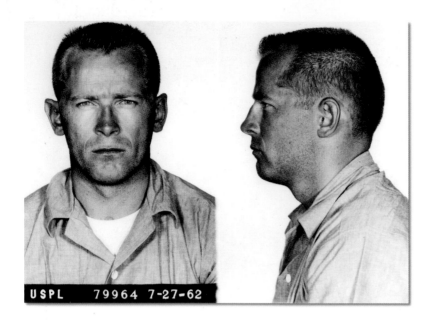

USPL 79964 7-27-62

DEPARTMENT OF JUSTICE
United States Penitentiary
Lewisburg, Pennsylvania
301 61 NE
9-4-63 JAMES J. BULGER, JR.

NARA

Bulger, above in July 1962, and in 1963 at Lewisburg, Pennsylvania, right, looking a bit more hopeful. He was released from Lewisburg penitentiary in 1965 and by then his hair had turned white.

borhood. His profits were not always at the expense of other criminals, however. Sometimes he swindled his own neighbors in Southie. In 1984 Julie and Stephen Rakes were allegedly forced at gunpoint to abandon their newly opened liquor store. Bulger moved in and used it as his base of operations. But even that story is mired in controversy, and marked by failed lawsuits, divorce and jail time. Rakes later lied about the takeover—allegedly out of fear that Bulger would harm him or his family—then was convicted of lying.

In another incident that shocked Massachusetts, it was revealed that in 1991 "Whitey" Bulger paid $700,000 in cash to the winner of the Massachusetts state lottery jackpot of $14.3 million in exchange for one-sixth of the winnings. Bulger needed a clean source of cash. He collected $119,408 a year until he was indicted and went underground in 1995. (The payout is 2010 and lawsuits have sprung up.)

But perhaps Whitey's most egregious series of crimes began in 1981 in Tulsa, Oklahoma with the killing of millionaire tech tycoon, Robert Wheeler.

Wheeler bought into the World Jai Alai franchise, which was said to be rife with Mafia money. Just as he was about to discover that one of his employees, John Callahan, was skimming a million a year off the top, he was fatally shot in the face at point blank range. Hit man, and government witness, John Martorano, confessed. Bulger and Flemmi had a meeting with Callahan and another hoodlum named Brian Halloran in which the murder was

discussed. In short order Callahan was killed. Hallaron became frantic and went on the run. He tried becoming an informant but was left dangling. One night he hitched a ride with a stranger and they were both murdered. Apparently Bulger got the word that Hallaron was trying to make a deal with the FBI. It's this series of murders and potential tip-offs that have caused agents Connolly and Rico their biggest troubles.

In reality, no one knows who pulled the triggers on the 18 victims "Whitey" Bulger is accused of killing—Flemmi, Weeks, Martorano, Bulger, or someone else—and in that regard Senator Bulger's assertion that crooks have been fingering his brother to save their own skins is plausible. But it is clear that killing was done and that "Whitey" Bulger was involved in it. And now a whole industry of accusations, denials, lottery claims, lawsuits, divorces, prison sentences, book deals, network and cable television shows and Hollywood movies have continued to titillate Massachusetts.

Yet Whitey was nowhere to be found. He and his girlfriend, Catherine Greig, disappeared just before the indictment and hightailed it across the country. They remained in Louisiana for several months and were conspicuous for their cash payouts to a poor family they befriended. It was reported early in his indictment and before he'd been in the news so often, that he was seen on Alcatraz showing a young couple his cell. There were sightings in New York, in Ireland and England. In early 2006, a senior citizen in a ball cap robbed a couple banks

Photograph by Officer William (Bill) Long, Jr.

Prisoners are released from their cells for early morning work at about the time Bulger served on Alcatraz.

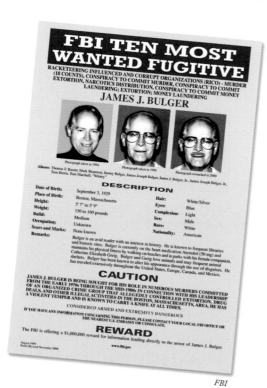

FBI

Captured $2 million man

in the Los Angeles metropolitan area.

So much time has elapsed, in fact, that John Martorano is out of prison after 12 years. And, as recent as November 2008, agent Connolly, who was already serving time for racketeering, was convicted of second degree murder.

Whitey, however, who has been featured on the television show *America's Most Wanted* many times, eluded capture until June 2011 when a woman recognized Catherine Greig from an FBI wanted anouncement on daytime television and called in the tip. Bulger was lured outside of his Santa Monica, California apartment and was arrested without incident. More than 30 weapons and more than $800,000 in cash was found in his apartment. Well connected, well financed and covered by his girlfriend, Bulger had remained undetected for 16 years. No doubt, she drove. Returned to Massachusetts, he will spend the rest of his life in prison. Greig, however, recently pled guilty in a bargain for a shorter sentence.

Stay tuned!

The Most Famous Escapees

Any listing of the most infamous prisoners on Alcatraz would not be complete without including the most famous men in the most provocative escape attempts.

Ralph Roe (1) and Teddy Cole (2) escaped on December 16, 1937. Their plan had been to depart on a foggy day. They broke through a window in old model industries building on the west side of the island, scrambled down the cliff and jumped into the San Francisco Bay. The bay's temperature at that time of year was about 55 degrees. Worse, they were swimming in the high-high tide which would lead them swiftly under the Golden Gate Bridge into the Pacific Ocean. Fog also hampered the rescue and they may have been lost at sea. Despite that they had no money, no crimes committed on land could be traced to them.

Frank Morris (3), Clarence and John Anglin (4 and 5) attempted escape on June 11, 1962 in one of the most sophisticated ruses in the prison's history. They dug through six inches of concrete to get into a utility corridor, then, leaving dummy masks in their beds, climbed the pipes to the ceiling, where they broke through a vent in the roof. They also made a raft out of raincoats. But like Roe and Cole, they departed on the high-high tide, and vanished without a trace on land.

Thirty-four men attempted escape in the prison's 29-year federal prison era. Seven were shot and killed, one drowned, five are still missing and the remaining were captured. But two men made it to shore.

In 1945, John Giles (6) surreptitiously put together an army sergeant's uniform from military laundry that came to the island's dock, then casually walked aboard an army boat that traveled from Angel Island to Alcatraz to San Francisco. Unfortunately, he boarded the boat that was heading to Angel Island instead of San Francisco. He was returned to Alcatraz within an hour where prison officers took his picture in his stolen uniform.

John Paul Scott (7) swam to San Francisco with the aid of surgical gloves tucked into prison shirt sleeves on December 16, 1962—the 25th anniversary of the Roe and Cole attempt. Scott floated for three miles and washed up on the rocks at Ft. Point, the old Army installation at the mouth of the Golden Gate Bridge. He was wearing only his shorts. Pulled off the rocks by a couple of kids who thought he was a bridge jumper, Scott was taken to a hospital where doctors revived him by warming his body temperature. It was a remarkable feat. But he was returned to the prison that night and photographed showing his cuts and bruises.

(Scott paroled out of prison in 1968, and for seven years was employed in an Atlanta, Georgia hospital as a laboratory technician. He also built houses, including his own ranch-style house. But something went awry and he robbed a bank at gun point, was convicted in 1977 and died in prison of leukemia in 1987 at age 61.)

Finally, Floyd Hamilton (8), who was linked to the notorious husband and wife team of Bonnie and Clyde, attempted escape with three others in April 1943. Hamilton was shot at and ducked into the water. Warden Johnston assumed he was dead but Hamilton swam back to the island, hid in a cave for three days and attempted—or thought about—swimming away. Eventually he gave up, climbed back up the cliff and broke into the model industries building. He was discovered sleeping next to the radiator. He's the only prisoner who tried to escape *into* Alcatraz.

Cover Design: Jolene Babyak
Front Cover photo courtesy of *AP/Wide World Photos*
Inside Back Cover from the
   Jack Fleming Collection GGNRA/PARC GOGA 3089
Book Design: Cory Kincade
Chapter Photos: Jolene Babyak
Printed in China by Global Interprint

Photo Credits

Photos are courtesy of the National Archives and Records Administration-Pacific Sierra Region and Washington, D.C. (NARA), the Betty Wallar, Mark Fischetti, Mike Mannion and Jack Fleming Alcatraz collections at the Golden Gate National Recreational Area Park Archives (GGNPR/PARC), Associated Press, Minnesota Historical Society, Minnesota Public Library, Federal Bureau of Investigation, Federal Bureau of Prisons, Chicago History Museum, San Francisco Public Library, Los Angeles Public Library, Alcatraz Alumni Association, Chuck Stucker, Anne Diestel, William "Bill" Long, Jr., George DeVincenzi, John Martini, Donald Bowden, Ed Faulk, Ann Collet, Philip F. Dollison and Corinne Dollison Edwards.

Sources for Further Reading

National Archives and Records Administration, Pacific Region, San Bruno, California: Record Group 129; Records of the Bureau of Prisons, Comprehensive Case Files of Alcatraz Inmates; *Alcatraz Island Prison*, James A. Johnston; *Black Mass*, Dick Lehr and Gerald O'Neill; *The Bulger Brothers: How They Terrorized and Corrupted Boston for a Quarter Century*, Howie Carr; *J. Edgar Hoover: The Man and His Secrets*, Curt Gentry; *John Dillinger Slept Here: A Crooks' Tour of Crime and Corruption in St. Paul, 1920-1936*, Paul MacCabee; *Machine Gun Kelly's Last Stand*, Stanley Hamilton; *Mean Men: The Sons of Ma Barker*, Robert Winter; *Mickey Cohen: In My Own Words*, Mickey Cohen; *Mr. Capone: The Real—and Complete—Story of Al Capone*, Robert J. Schoenberg; *On Doing Time*, Morton Sobell; *On the Rock: 25 Years on Alcatraz*, Alvin Karpis; *Public Enemies*, Bryan Burrough; *Public Enemies: America's Criminal Past*, William Helmer; *Roy Gardner: My Story*, Roy Gardner; FBI files of "Doc" Barker, George Kelly, Mickey Cohen and the 1939 Escape from Alcatraz.

Acknowledgements

The author wishes to thank Nicki Phelps, Kathy Hoggard, Dianna Waggoner, Tess Eisley, Polly Pettit, Anne Diestel, Rick Peuser, Regalle Asuncion, Joseph Sanchez, Rose Mary Kennedy, Philip F. Dollison, John and Betsy Martini, Chuck Stucker, two former Alcatraz officers—William "Bill" Long, Jr. and George DeVincenzi—who are good photographers, Roxane Buck-Ezcurra, Linda "Sam" Haskins, Susan Tasaki, David Bullen, Vivian Young, Michael Blaustone, Susan Ewing Haley, Amanda Williford, Pam Whitman, M.A., who first suggested that "Creepy" Karpis may have had Asperger's Syndrome, Al Blank, Robert Lieber, Chris Warren, Milagros "La La" Macapagal, LuLu Sera, John Moran, Art Owen, special mention to D'Marco Parrilla, Vic Balauat, Jason Irby and Kristen Elford, as well as Sara Sanderson, Mariah Weaver, Cathy Dollison Brandt and Lexi Brandt.

Cory Kincade is the pen name of Jolene Babyak, who lived on Alcatraz as a child. Author of *Eyewitness on Alcatraz, Birdman: The Many Faces of Robert Stroud* and *Breaking the Rock: The Great Escape from Alcatraz*, she has become an authority on Alcatraz and its inhabitants through research and interviews.

You May Wish to Order These Books

Eyewitness On Alcatraz, $12.95 US
Birdman: The Many Faces of Robert Stroud, $13.95 US
Breaking the Rock: The Great Escape from Alcatraz, $14.95 US
Alcatraz Most Wanted, $10.95 US

Ariel Vamp Press
High Tart Productions
P.O. Box 3496
Berkeley, CA 94703